Jack's Story

First Published 2015

Bretwalda Books, Unit 8, Fir Tree Close, Epsom, Surrey KT17 3LD
info@BretwaldaBooks.com
www.BretwaldaBooks.com
ISBN 978-1-910440-06-3

Printed and bound in Great Britain by
Marston Book Services Ltd, Oxfordshire

Jack's Story

by
Alan Pack

Chapter One

She woke me at ten minutes past midnight.

And now the dog was making her way downstairs before I had time to get myself out of bed and onto my feet. In a half comatose state I stumbled after her, pulling on a sweatshirt and the first footwear that came to hand as I went, I was already part dressed in tracky bottoms, which I had been sleeping in, because when there is a pregnant bitch in the house you have no idea what time of day or night she will start to give birth, and need to be ready to follow her at anytime, anywhere which includes outside into the garden in case she tries to give birth out there. So a torch that works is also a part of the essential kit that needs to be to hand, as most births in the animal kingdom happen at night. This is because there are fewer predators around in the wild at night and untold thousands of years in domestication have not altered that natural instinct.

I had taken the week off work so as to be around when she went into labour. She had been mated exactly sixty-three days ago. Going on how she was acting yesterday, I had convinced myself she was no nearer to giving birth than I was, and had talked myself into going to work today. Because a bitch does not necessarily conceive on the day of mating as the sperm can remain live in her uterus for up to a week, the sixty three days is therefore only a guide. You can usually tell if a bitch is pregnant by the subtle changes in her behaviour long before medical science is able to give confirmation. But Tasha had not given any signs whatsoever. It was only after an ultrasound scan by the vet on day forty that I had any idea she was actually carrying puppies at all.

She had gone downstairs to look for a safe haven to give birth, and made a direct beeline for the brick lined cubbyhole in the alcove by the chimney breast, the most inaccessible spot in the whole house, but where she often took refuge and used to go to sleep there sometimes when she did not want to be disturbed, and no doubt looked upon as the safest place available. All the other dogs, sensing something was afoot, followed us.

I practically had to prise her out of there; she had made her mind up that this is where she wanted to be to have her family, and that was that. Taking Tasha by the collar I coaxed her back up the stairs and into the whelping box which had been set up for her in the back bedroom, closing the door behind us to prevent any of the others following. She had been shown the whelping box before to try and get her used to it, but like any pregnant female, she had her own ideas about where she was going to give birth.

By now my drowsiness had evaporated and my sluggish responses had sharpened tenfold, as they do when faced with an emergency situation such as this. While this may be just nature taking its course, I needed to be alert and fully functioning for what was about to come, just in case.

Ten minutes later she had given birth to the first puppy, a gold boy. I had always wanted a gold girl, but there were still others to come, so fingers crossed. I have not had a gold puppy for the last two litters, so I just might be lucky this time around, because this line seems to be prone to boys and usually blacks.

She went on to give birth to a further four puppies, one of these was still born, and despite all efforts of blowing into its muzzle, swinging it in a downward motion and rubbing it with a towel, I couldn't start it breathing. It was already dead. This happens sometimes and there is nothing more I could do about it other than what I had already tried. It is a fact of life. Innocence eternal.

Dog breeding is not all plain sailing, for the reason just given, and you never get what you want in terms of colour and sex. As I have said I would have liked a gold girl, but that was not to be. I had a black female with a big white patch on her chest. White is allowed on the chest in a cocker, but a lot of judges do not like any at all. All the others were boys. Girls are easier to sell because of their breeding potential, and are consequently more valuable. They also have a very placid outlook to life and are easier to train than boys, who, certainly in cockers, can tend to be very self-willed, although in their defence they can be very attentive when it suits. That just has to co-incide with your wishes.

When she had settled to suckling them, I went down stairs to see to the others and get all our breakfasts. This included Tasha; I took her bowl of food up to her, she abandoned her new family whilst she ate her food and was a bit reluctant to return to them, but she got there in the end and settled down again to stay with her pups after some coaxing from me.

Tasha was a little nervous of the pups because this was her first litter; she was a bit bewildered with the new arrivals, and what she was supposed to do with them. Though she had followed her instincts so far, when they were born she had given birth very easily, the labour had not been difficult, like shelling peas. She had chewed off the umbilical cords herself and licked them dry but like her Mother had not bothered to eat the afterbirths, so I disposed of those for her. Now she was feeding them as long as I stayed with her, but she was reluctant to stay with her new family on her own. She would go for so long and then follow me downstairs, frightened she was missing something maybe. I then had to take her back up to them and sit with her until she drifted off to sleep with the pups snuggled up to her for warmth, and quietly sneak back down the stairs. I did finally manage to get her to stay on her own after a few days of persuasive coaxing to settle her to the task in hand.

By this time I would usually be phoning a vet to arrange for them to be docked. But the law had changed earlier that year and this was no longer legal except for dogs where it could be proven they were destined to work as gundogs. You can no longer show a docked dog that was born after 6 April 2007. When I first came to Cockers my original pair were docked. I had not really given the matter much thought as to whether I agreed with the procedure or not. I suppose I sat on the fence having been brought up in a generation where all gundogs were docked. I watched my grandfather dock a litter for someone with a pair of household scissors, mind you he kept them razor sharp and he did a wonderful job, there was not a drop of blood. He wanted me to go into the house so I would not see what was happening, but the usual childhood curiosity took over, so I stayed put. It was legal then for anyone to dock dogs providing it was done before their eyes were open.

Then the law was changed and only a vet could do the procedure, and the puppies had to be less than three days old. Not all vets would do it, because as usual the law was vaguely worded and it depended on how the reader interpreted the "as necessary" bit of the legislation. You had to belong to this club to get a list of vets near to you who would dock, and most of these also required you to be either one of their clients or a member of this club. I had to drive forty miles to my nearest participating vet, and because the pups were so young they had to go with their Mother. The ambient temperature of the car also had to be kept constant, equal to what they were used to in the house, because pups cannot maintain their own internal body temperature when this young. It was quite a clat really, because two people had to go so one could be with the Mother and pups to look after them. The pups had to be taken in to the vet in small groups, so that the Mother was never left alone without any of them and would hopefully not become too stressed if some went missing for a short time, which could have led to the possibility of her abandoning them. You always held the pup; the vet did not touch them so that there was no transfer of any strange smells onto them for when they were put back with their Mother. He also removed the dew claws from the front feet, which is like a thumb on the insides of the front legs, and is no longer of use to the dog. Something evolution has deemed is not needed anymore but which could be snagged and broken when out hunting if not taken off. Kathleen had taken hers to a vet to be docked, so I was not going to let any reservations I may want to have about docking stand between me and two lovely dogs. It has only been since that the non breeding, non shooting, don't get out of bed in case you break a nail brigade, has stuck its oar in that the law has now altered again.

So now the tail has to remain full length. I have seen some really bad examples on cockers, and because up to now all of mine have been docked, I don't know if I have just been lucky here, but the pups have really good looking tails and carry them well. The tail can at times be handy for other things than wagging and causing a draft. For example when brushing the animal if the dog tries to get away it is handy to grab as a last resort to try and stop the attempt, an option not previously available to Cocker owners, unless you were quick that is. Full tails can also cause problems; a dog will be sat near something and wag their tail and as it knocks, they will bark at the knocking, and then wag their tail again because they are happy to be barking and then bark at the knocking again and thus starts a vicious circle. Jack will stand near the cooker and beat his tail against it to a rhythm not unlike the Red Indians when holding a war council, and who knows maybe that is what he is calling for over the feeding arrangements or something else he is not happy with. As I keep pointing out, if they are unhappy with any of the arrangements – they know where the door is.

Tasha is the daughter of Nikita (Niki) and Granddaughter of her Mother, Sweep. Sooty and Sweep were my first two dogs, litter sisters, bought from a Lady in Norfolk. The purchase was funded by the money from my Grandfather's will. He used to breed Cockers and it was this that first attracted me to the breed. And by keeping the line going I feel that I have some kind of continuing connection to him. He would turn in his grave if he knew how much I had paid for them, but he would have loved them when he recovered from the shock of the cost.

When I went to pick out the two I wanted they were just six weeks old, I had the choice of four girls from a litter of six all black puppies. I had phoned Kathleen before the litter were born and she had taken my phone number and said she would phone me back after they had arrived. She phoned a few days after the birth and told me there were two boys and four girls; she described the litter and said there was one small one and one with a white star on the chest. I had the choice from all four girls because the boys were already spoken for.

Kathleen Cannelll was eighty years of age when I met her. She had a lovely soft Norfolk accent which is one of my favourites. No offence to the Scots, but I spent a week in Edinburgh and could not make much sense of anything that was said to me. I really struggled with the accent up there and had to listen very carefully to everything that was said to me to have even half a chance of understanding it, and usually ended up deciphering the meaning from the number of syllables. They also use their own bank notes. I travelled up by train and having not much else to do, I had taken to studying the racing page. Spotting one of those winners that cannot lose, when I walked off the station towards the hotel I had booked into, I went into the first bookies I came across. When I checked later in the day the horse had "come home", so I went to the counter to claim my winnings and was paid out. I turned to leave when I looked at the money I had been given, these were funny looking notes and turned back to the counter and was about to protest because if you are going to get a dodgy note from anywhere it could well be a bookmaker, when it clicked just before I had got my mouth into gear that these were Scottish notes. Having averted the disaster of making a complete fool of myself I turned back towards the door and left.

Kathleen was badly afflicted with arthritis, and walked very slowly and with great difficulty, using two sticks. She had seven dogs that I saw, and had raised a litter of puppies. Hats off to her because keeping one Cocker can be a handful when half her age, let alone seven of them. And raising a litter of puppies is no walk in the park. She had a heart of gold and loved her dogs. She would do anything to help anyone in Cockers, and loved to be kept up to date with those of her own breeding's progress.

Using a cardboard box to carry them out of the bedroom where they were with their Mother, she brought the four girls out and I helped her to carry them into the kitchen. I picked them up one by one to look at them. The little one nibbled at my finger as I held her. She wanted to be put back in the box with her litter mates. In desperation she gave my thumb a hard nip and wriggled and squeaked until she got what she wanted. A little fighter this one, who was not going to stand for any nonsense.

I had more or less made my mind up before I arrived there that my choice was going to be the little one and the one with the white. Not the best of methods when picking out a puppy that was going to be the foundation of future breeding. But at this point that was not a consideration. When they had been returned to their Mother I accepted the offer of a welcome cup of tea. She gave me a list of what I would need to get before they were taken to their new home, like the type of food they were using, she also showed me the size of basket I would need so they could lay stretched out in it and also a couple of brushes I would be needing to keep their coats in order. I paid her a deposit as we had agreed, and left. It had started to pour with rain so I saw myself out of the gate as I didn't want her to get soaked. She was very concerned that I closed the gate properly. I assured her I would and made certain I did, I did not want to be responsible for any escapees. I couldn't wait until I would be able to collect them which would be when they were eight weeks. We agreed that I would fetch them on the Sunday when they would actually be eight and a half weeks old. She seemed concerned that they stayed with their Mother as long as possible. My Dad had agreed he would drive me there to collect them, so I could be in the back of the car with the pups in an open cardboard box, and be able to look after them.

Some will advise against the purchase of two dogs together, especially from the same litter, and from my personal experience this holds to be very true. They will be more inclined to bond with each other sooner than you. If you want two the best thing is to get the one to start with and then the other about three months later, after the first one has had the chance to become settled and trained. In subsequent litters I have bred myself and kept two, the same problem arises.

In my defence, my excuse for going against this advice is I wanted two together because I would be going out to work, and I did not want to leave one on its own. My place of work was close enough to be able to come home at lunch times so they would not be left all day on their own. The best combination if you are contemplating having two dogs is a boy and a girl, but obviously you can get problems when the bitch comes into season. And it is no use hoping that the dog will not be mature enough when she first comes into season, as a bitch will usually mature before the dog, but she could also be late with her first season.

The next best combination is two girls. Two boys can be prone to fight and be a handful at the best of times, especially if they are litter brothers, but how things actually work out is very much down to the individual personalities of the dogs involved, regardless of breed.

In other respects a pair together does make things easier. They will play with each other and amuse each other. It stops them becoming too "humanised" , as a single pup will tend to, seeming to forget it is a dog, and a lone dog needs a lot more of your attention which it will be constantly seeking, especially at the very start.

I had already built a kennel and pen in the back garden, and now I had a shopping list made up of puppy food, cornflakes, Cow and Gate baby milk and eggs, all to get in time for their arrival. Breakfast was made up of tinned puppy food (meat), a hardboiled egg and cornflakes all soaked in warm milk and mixed together. Looked disgusting to me, but they ate it and seemed to enjoy it, so that was all that mattered. This took time to get ready, so to save a bit of time in the morning I tried cooking the egg the night before. Next morning at breakfast they wouldn't touch it. So bang went that theory. The egg had to be freshly done, and waiting for a hardboiled egg to cool that has spent the last ten or so minutes in boiling water seemed to take forever and a day, not helped by two demanding puppies wanting breakfast now! What I do with pups now if I am in a hurry in the morning is they get their "breakfast" with the egg etc at their tea time meal, when I have more time to prepare the concoction, and the egg can be cooked about half an hour earlier to give it time to cool down or alternatively cooked at dinner time and left to cool. The shorter time lapse between cooking and serving seems to be acceptable to the young connoisseurs of fine English breakfast cuisine.

Having walked round the perimeter fence of the garden checking for possible escape routes, and blocking them all up, or so I thought, I would have put money on the fact that it was escape proof. I had bought a book on Cocker Spaniels and there was a chapter entitled "Your first puppy" with a picture of a man with a cocker puppy in his arms which he needed both of them to hold the dog with. When I saw them at six weeks they were really tiny and you could sit them one on each hand with ease. I did not really give the matter a second thought and when they came home at eight and a half weeks they were not that much bigger, and certainly a lot smaller than the one in the book, so before I dare let them out into the garden I had to rush round again and bung up all the holes I had ignored the first time round because I thought they were too small for a pup to get through. There are two types of Cocker, the working and show. Cockers from show lines do have a tendency to be smaller than those from a working strain anyway.

I went with my Dad to collect them on that Sunday afternoon. It was a lovely warm, but not too hot, sunny afternoon for September. The perfect temperature for transporting puppies in a car. Up until today I had been really excited, just like a child anticipating Christmas, but now we were on the way to fetch them, a rising panic had begun to kick in. Was I doing the right thing? Would I be able to look after them properly? It was too late to change my mind now, but that did not stop the panic rising like the mercury on the hottest day of the year. Had I been driving I might well have done a U- turn and gone home again.

When we arrived Kathleen had already separated them from the rest of the litter and they were happily playing with each other on the floor in the front room, totally oblivious of the big change that was about to take place in their young and so far short little lives, and so engrossed in their game that they ignored our arrival altogether. We sorted out all the paperwork over a cup of tea, including the payment of the balance. One of the adult dogs, a big black male came into the lounge and took a look at the pups, he had a sniff of them both before he returned to the kitchen. He obviously did not do children.

Kathleen gave both of them a final cuddle goodbye with tears in her eyes. This must have been really hard for her to see them go despite having done so countless times before with former litters. We assured her they would be well looked after, and with that, I put them into the cardboard box we had taken with us for them to ride home in, took them out of the bungalow and put them onto the back seat of the car where I sat beside them. Kathleen came out to the car to see them settled and watch us drive off.

Now I was the proud owner of two lovely Cocker Spaniel puppies. The journey home was about forty minutes on a fairly fast road, and with it being Sunday afternoon there was little traffic around, so nothing hindered our progress. The dog with the white went to sleep in a corner of the box and that was where she stayed, contentedly curled up there all the way home, while the little all black kept poking her head over the top of the box for a look round sniffing inquisitively at the air, we had one of the windows open because it was a little warm, so probably all sorts of new exciting smells were drifting passed her muzzle. Some dogs will keep standing up for a look at the world going by when they are travelling. It is probably for the same reason that some people have to sit at the front of a bus so they can see where they are going or else they feel travel sick.

When we arrived home I put them in the pen while I got myself organised. At first they could not negotiate the step up at the back door because they were so tiny, so I had to make a half step for them so that they could get in and out by themselves. I improvised with some lengths of 4X4 I found in the garage which they took to using straight away. They were not so keen on the latticed decking I made for them later when I had the time, which would have felt strange to their paws at first, and they tried their level best to leap over it and avoid having to stand on it. They came round to using it in a few days.

I had decided in the interim between selecting the two I wanted and going to fetch them, after several weeks of toying with different names and rejecting silly suggestions from work colleagues which included Spot and Snowy, to call them Sooty and Sweep. These were the only two names that I could think of in the two and a half weeks I had to make my mind up, that went together as well as meaning black. Kathleen had asked if I had decided on names while we were talking, and when I told her what I had thought of, she agreed that Sooty would suit the all black dog, so she must have looked like a Sooty. When naming a dog, consider this scenario. You have lost the dog in a crowd, would you scream its name out at the top of your voice? If the answer is no, then think again.

I was anticipating problems when I tried to teach them their individual names because of having acquired the two together I was thinking that it would be difficult for each dog to grasp who was who, certainly to begin with anyway. But surprisingly without any extra effort on my part, they seemed to cotton on surprisingly easily to which name referred to which dog. Mind when the prospect of food is in the offing they will respond to any name you care to call, which is a world of difference to when they are out in the field hunting a scent and you want them to come back. Then it is a case of one saying to the other, "Did you hear something?" and the other replying, "No. Definitely not. Just keep going!"

And another problem with keeping two or more dogs at any given time, the more frantically distraught the owner's calls for obedience become. My Mother is a case in point. Now they have two dogs, when I phone up there is a more frequent shouting in the background as one or the other is doing something they shouldn't.

My rising panic was still going in one direction only, and that was up. All of a sudden I was totally in charge of two puppies. We had kept dogs before, but now I was on my own, if anything went wrong, it was going to be down to me and me alone. Their health and wellbeing was entirely in my hands, a responsibility that can only be likened possibly to having a first baby. For a whole week I was unable to keep my breakfast down because of nerves, my stomach was just churning. I felt like a duck out of water despite all my experience with dogs, which right at this moment seemed grossly inadequate.

Puppies very quickly become trusting to their new owner. They look to you to feed them, walk them, care for them and give them all the love and affection they need. A week after Sooty and Sweep had arrived I was going to wash the blanket that had been in the bottom of the box they came home in, and they both ran to it and inspected it, vigorously sniffing it, I expect they recognised the smell it must have picked up on it from what they would still probably refer to as home.

I had taken a fortnights leave to get them settled into their new home and also to get them used to being in the kennel on their own for a part of the day. I introduced them to this by putting them into the pen and going out to fetch the newspaper. On cue they started to cry and whimper. But they would have to get used to this routine, so I ignored them and carried on to the shop. If I had gone back they would assume that crying was all they had to do to stop me leaving them every time I tried to go out on my own, so I turned a deaf ear and just carried on going. I was only gone ten minutes and when I returned, they were still crying, I came in the gate and said to them "That wasn't very good was it?" and left it at that.

The next day I repeated the same routine, but this time I left them for an hour. I needed to get them to four hours and the quicker we could get there the better. Next door said they had started to cry as I had first left, but had soon settled down. One thing you need when starting out with new pups is understanding neighbours. Or alternatively one that is hard of hearing. Fred and Molly had popped round the previous day just after we had got home for a quick look at the new arrivals; I think they were possibly keener than I was at this point. Sooty and Sweep now seemed to realise that I would be coming back and they just had to be patient and wait. I kept extending the time I left them, by half an hour at a time, until I got them to all morning, which is what I would need. I bought them a clock to help try and settle them, the ticking gives them a sound to listen to and they do not feel totally lonely, and no, not so they can tell what time it is! But finding one that had a loud tick these days took some doing, I had all the shops selling bedside clocks in town winding them up for me to see how loud they ticked. I eventually found one in the most expensive shop in town. Typical that. Another trick is to leave them with a radio playing quietly so that there is something making a noise while they are on their own, mind you, you need to be careful of the station you leave them listening to, especially with young impressionable puppies!

Our very first dog was a Beagle cross named Lucky. So called because she was a stray who had latched herself onto my Dad and the men he was working with shortly after New Year. They were working in a remote part of the fens and she hung around because the men fed her from their sandwiches, probably the first square-ish meal she had seen in days, and she kept appearing every day around meal times; obviously an unwanted Christmas present; abandoned and now with nowhere else to go. By the end of the week my Dad took her to the police station to register her as a lost dog, and asked if he could bring her home. Because she was a smallish dog he thought she would be good to get my brother used to dogs. Ian did not like dogs at all and would give any he met in the street a very wide berth, even to the detriment of road safety. With it being January, when she came in under my Dad's arm, she leapt from his grasp and made a bee-line straight for the real fire, and had soon pushed her way to the front; warmth, at last. She had to make do with the scraps left over from tea for a meal, fortunately Mum had bought an extra large piece of meat that day. She soon polished that off with some vegetables. Fed as well, this was heaven. And a walk also thrown in, could this get any better?

She had to make do with a lot of make shift arrangements as her arrival was unexpected. She slept in the shed until a kennel had been built for her. That took several weekends of us working in the snow to get it finished for her, and ironically on the weekend it was done and ready, she had had a "rough house" that night in the shed by knocking all the contents westward. She also had to make do with make shift food and water bowls. My brother bought her a proper water bowl with "Dog" on the front. That was until my Mother dropped it; then it read "og". And was no longer any use as a bowl anyway.

Seven days after her arrival the police called to say she had not been claimed and gave us the paper work to say she was ours if we wanted her, otherwise they would take her now and put her to sleep. That still happened then, if a dog was not claimed in seven days. And since that day our periods without a dog have only been brief while a replacement has been sought after the predecessors passing.

I left it a few days before phoning Mrs Cannell to let her know that Sooty and Sweep were getting on just fine in their new home. I did not want to ring her too early with a list of questions in case it appeared that I did not know how to look after them, but I don't think she would have thought that at all. She would have been more than happy to help, but I just felt self conscious about appearing incapable. When I did phone I think she was pleased to hear from me because she said a lot of people did not bother, but when all said and done they were her babies and I think she should be kept informed of their progress. She cleared up a few points of concern I had about puppies. Periodically I would get a photo reprinted and send it to her with a letter bringing her up to date on their latest antics, because as they got older they certainly became wiser. If you breed them, the pups quickly pick up on all the tricks of the trade off the adults before then going on to invent new ones of their own. Then the adults pick up on the best of those, and so it goes on.

House training a Cocker is not too arduous a task but does require patience, which can wear fairly thin at times. I had tried for days to get Sooty and Sweep to use newspaper for spending a penny on, but they preferred to use their own chosen spots, although Mrs Cannelll had said they were already trained to using paper, they were not showing any signs of obliging to remember. At the time I had a pre-dog habit of putting the TV guide on the floor by my chair so that it was always handy. One time I had done this as usual, and the next time I went to pick it up it was all wet. One of them had done a penny on it, I jumped up to protest and there they sat looking at me, and you could read their minds "You said on the paper!"

Generally a Cocker picks up the idea to go outside pretty quickly, but then about two weeks later it is as if they get bored with asking and revert to cocking their leg anywhere half handy again, just because it is far easier. Boys will cock their legs against table legs and anything else vertical, this includes your leg if you stand still for long enough given half the chance, particularly when they have an in season bitch in the house, and when this occurs I keep finding little puddles all over the place. And if you have several dogs they all have to mark the spot, and the little puddle quickly becomes a great lake!

With Sooty and Sweep I would leave the back door open so that they could go out if they needed to while I went up stairs to clean my teeth and have a shave. While I was gone, every morning one of them kept leaving a little parcel in the middle of the lounge carpet. Because I did not see the culprit I could not really make too much fuss about it, but made it plain that I was not happy and kept giving Sooty a hard stare because I was convinced it was her as she was always the one that looked the guiltiest. One morning I had run out of toothpaste, so I came back down to get a fresh tube from the cupboard under the kitchen sink. I caught Sweep in the middle of the act. I scooped her up and dumped her roughly on the back lawn. Sooty gave a yelp, ran outside and promptly did a penny on the lawn as if to say "look, I am a good girl". That was the last time I found any unwanted parcels on the carpet. They hate being in trouble but this does not deter them from being mischievous.

Training a Cocker is a bit like a see-saw game of give and take. You give the commands, they take liberties. You think you are training them, but what is really happening is they are bringing you round, subtly, to their line of thinking. They can be very attentive to you if it is convenient to be so, but otherwise, especially if you have more than one out with you, they are going to do what they want first. It is like they are goading each other to see who is going to respond last. How many lively self willed Cockers do you see in obedience? In an attempt to get Sooty and Sweep to respond to the recall, or at least to keep an eye on how far in front of me they were getting instead of just ploughing ahead regardless, I tried hiding behind a brick built tunnel entrance, they did eventually notice that I was nowhere to be seen and ventured back to see where I had got to. I don't think it had much success at getting them to pay more attention to me though.

Cockers not only need love, attention and walking, they also need regular grooming and clipping to keep their coats in good order and avoid cots and matts in their fur. I started off with a few combs and brushes, and then I would see something I thought might be useful, buy it to give it a go, and before I knew where I was I have ended up with quite a paraphernalia of various tools, combs and brushes etc. These consequently all needed keeping somewhere and I have bought various tool boxes which have got steadily bigger as the years have gone by to accommodate my ever growing collection. A toolbox is handy to keep everything together and just grab to take to a show, because I never know what I might need with me, like when I am going to find a knot in one or the other's coat; it is also good if I am in a real hurry on a show morning, which is often the case, when I have not had time to groom them prior to going, because then I can do a quick tidy up at ringside knowing I will have everything to hand.

One really big frustration on acquiring a new puppy is that to begin with you can't take it out for a walk until it has had all its vaccinations. After all that is one of the reasons you own a dog for, to take it for a walk, otherwise you may as well keep a goldfish. (No offence intended to the aquatic enthusiasts out there, I do keep goldfish myself). I had bought two puppy collar and lead sets for Sooty and Sweep along with all the other paraphernalia they needed on arrival, and walked them round the cul-de-sac to get them used to being on a lead and going out for a walk. There were no other dogs that walked round there at the time, so they were unlikely to pick any infections up. I did this because one dog we had, asked and asked to be taken out, and when she could, she suddenly just did not want to know.

In the meantime they were quite contented with playing amongst themselves in the back garden which they had soon laid claim to as their own. A cat used to cross over the garden on his way home, which was okay with me, but not with Sooty and Sweep. Sooty in particular. She hated cats. And it seems to be a trait with Cockers, or this line in particular anyway, because I do know of people who keep a Cocker and a cat. Sooty would go boo loo if she saw one and would not rest until she had seen it off and it was out of sight. The one that crossed the garden would sit and wait on the other side of the fence until he had checked they were both inside and the coast was clear, then I would see him make his move and scoot over the opposite fence into his own garden and safety. Until Sooty asked to go out one night and caught him half way across her lawn, he left via the six foot rear fence without touching it. Sooty right behind him only just managed to pull herself up before she made an aperture in the fences woodwork approximately her size. And this trait seems to have been passed down the line, because none of them will tolerate the sight of their feline arch rivals.

When they did finally get to go out for their first walk, they trotted along the road quite well together as they were keen to keep up with each other, and I think with there being the two of them they helped boost each other's confidences. When one stopped she quickly sniffed whatever and came galloping after her sister well before the leads became taught between them, or else the other would double back to see what her sibling was finding so interesting. When they came home they had a treat each and promptly curled up for a sleep. Tired out, but displaying contentment at its best.

Sooty could be a bit of a bully, as far as she was concerned she was the boss, and Sweep did not make any attempt to dispute this, she just accepted the arrangement. At times Sooty would get into the kennel first and not let Sweep in, who would curl herself up in the pen yard. While this was sort of okay whilst it was warm weather, I was not entirely happy with the situation, I did not like to think Sweep was being pushed out all the time by Sooty, although when I came home they were both in the kennel so she had got herself in there at some point or another. I had to creep into the house really quietly so they were not aware I was home, because the minute they heard me they would coming bowling out of the kennel and start barking with excitement - "He's back". I had started to scour all the books I had on animal behaviour to try and find a solution. Although I needn't have worried, Sweep was one step in front of me, she had a cunning plan of her own to get into the kennel. When Sooty was in one of those moods, Sweep would stand in the kennel yard barking. After a short time, curiosity would get the better of Sooty, and she came bowling out to see what it was her sister was barking at, and while she was stood there looking round for whatever all the fuss was about, Sweep would nip behind her and get herself settled in the best place on the duvet. I had put an old duvet in there as a bed for them to snuggle up in and keep warm if it was cold. A spell outside even when it is cold will help a dog maintain a healthy thick coat. If they are indoors all the time in central heating, their coats can become thin, they tend to moult more frequently and to be prone to scurf from flaky skin.

Puppies will pick up new ideas very quickly, for example, they soon learn to climb stairs, but then arises the problem of how to get back down again because they have to come head first, and until they have mastered the technique, they have to be carried down. It does not usually take them long to sort themselves out and soon grasp the idea with a bit of coaxing. In most cases that is. Sweep always made out she could not come down stairs, though her sister, who was never keen on being carried at the best of times and liked to do things for herself anyway, had picked up the knack quite quickly. She was a very independent little soul. If there are other adult dogs around it takes even less time because the pups just copy them.

I was installing a smoke alarm on the landing and had the small step ladder across the top of the stairs, I knew I had one dog in the bedroom and the other one down stairs, but I did not know which way round they were. As I was working a dog came up the stairs and hesitated at the ladder and decided to go back down, that must be Sooty as Sweep could still not get down stairs on her own. Anyway after a short while, the dog whom I had assumed to be Sooty, came up the stairs again, and this time braved passing under the ladder. She turned and looked up at me and it was then that I caught sight of the white on the chest. This was Sweep. Now just a minute, that meant she had gone down the stairs on her own. She had been having me on all this time whilst I was gullible enough to carry her. Well that was going to stop. I don't know about other breeds, but Cockers are always one and a half steps in front of you and will take full advantage at every single opportunity that comes their way. Sweep was very quickly becoming a master.

I went downstairs and Sooty came down behind me. Sweep stood stubbornly at the top of the stairs and started to cry and whimper because she wanted me to fetch her. I left her. This was going to be a battle of wills, who was going to give in first? Had I not seen her come down the stairs on her own just minutes earlier, it would have most likely been me. After ten minutes of getting nowhere she decided to relent and came down on her own. Anyway it was dinner time and she was in danger of missing out on her milk and chew. One to me; a rare occurrence. She tried a similar trick once pretending to have a limp when she was out on a walk. Well to give her her due, it may have started off as genuine. But if I was daft enough to carry her she was not going to stop me. After carrying her some distance, I had to put her down for a few minutes, and as she walked off she was limping on the other leg, and for a few moments I had to check that I was right, yes, it was definitely the other leg. She gave up trying after a short time when it was obvious she had milked that one to the full and was not going to get any more sympathy or another carry from me.

Mrs Cannelll was always willing to advise on any problems that arose, and did not make me feel inadequate no matter how trivial my concern was, she also made me feel at ease to ask her in the first place and not that I was incapable of looking after one of her dogs. She helped pick Niki out of Sweep's litter. By the time Toby and Tasha came along she had lost all of her dogs and was not well. In the latter few months she went into a rest home. I took Sooty and Sweep to see her. She did not recognise me or them. Sweep recognised her, but was confused as to why she was not responding to her and kept coming to me with a questioning expression. This was more than I could bear and we left as soon as we reasonably could. I do not cope very well at all with this sort of thing and find it easier to avoid if at all possible, the ostrich approach, but feel for anyone that does not have any choice in the matter. I was also worried about Sweep and what effect it was having on her. Sooty did not show her emotions as obviously as her sister did, she is a very private little dog who keeps them under wraps, but that is not to say she doesn't have feelings. Just more adept at not letting them show. This makes her more of a difficult dog to read.

Somewhere between Toby and Tasha and the arrival of Jack and Arran, Mrs Cannelll died. I am not very good with funerals at the best of times either, and this was definitely not one of those. I kept welling up inside and the hymn book was just a blur swimming in front of me through a sea of tears. I had only agreed to go because her daughter had phoned and asked if I would be going. It had always been on the cards that Sooty and Sweep would out live her. I took a little posy of flowers, dedicating it from Danehouse's Dinky and Delfie (their registered names) because anyone there reading the card would not have known "Sooty and Sweep" from Adam. I decided on the caption "In your passing, thank you for our gift of life".

Chapter Two

Sweep was always willing to get involved with new born pups, her maternal instincts were very strong, she made an excellent surrogate Mum and always showed willing to lend a paw when there were pups around. She had helped Niki with Tasha and Toby and was keen to assist now. But Tasha was not having any of it, no matter how well intended the help that was offered, so Sweep was just going to have to take a back seat until her granddaughter's pups were up on their feet and running around and Tasha's Mothering instincts had began to wane.

I buried the still born pup in the garden underneath the laurel bushes. This was not too difficult to deal with, because I had not had any opportunity to bond with the animal, but it is still sad because it is a life that never really started. And all life is precious. So fragile, and can be snatched away from you in a nanosecond, and there is nothing you can do to bring it back. It affects all of us – none of us are immortal. The essence of life is life itself and should be preserved at all costs, especially in the innocent like here where the chance to be otherwise is just so cruelly snatched away.

All the litter had started to suckle except for one. A red boy. That first feed is all important because the Mother's milk known as colostrum contains antibodies that give the pups the protection they need against all the little bugs the Mother has encountered. Without that inside them you are fighting a losing battle, as was proven with Sweep's first litter, and no substitute milk can duplicate the Mother's. The pup would not pass anything either, so he was not formed properly inside. He fortunately soon died which was a blessing as he was not going to make it, and that was another grave by the laurel bushes.

So we were left with three pups, the red and black boys, and the black girl with the white chest.

Because of Tasha's unwillingness to be on her own I moved her into the bedroom beside my bed so that I could at least try to get some sleep tonight, and would stand a better chance of hearing her or the pups if she rolled on one in the night, which a bitch can do and sometimes with fatal consequences. A "pig rail" as it is known allows the pups to get out of the way of their Mother if she is moving around, it runs round three sides of the whelping box giving them something to take sanctuary under to prevent her crushing them, although it is not a guarantee. Some Mothers in the wild move their young shortly after giving birth so that the smell of the afterbirth does not attract the attention of unwanted predators. This was the second time I had moved a bitch and her pups within one or two days of giving birth, and the bitch involved always seemed to settle better afterwards.

In the early hours of the next morning I woke, and for a while in a half dazed state, lay staring at something black on one of the bean beds. It took quite some time for it to register that it was one of the pups. When my brain had kicked into gear, I leapt out of bed and picked it up. It was the girl. She was very cold. Tasha had put her out in the night. A bitch will sometimes do this; like any wild animal, the Mother will not waste time on a pup if she has any reason to suspect it will not make it. She must have sensed something was wrong with her and did not want to waste any energy on feeding her. I scooped her up and put her back into the whelping box to get warmth from her Mother's body. Tasha did not object to her being replaced, but I had no idea how long she had been away from the nest.

Tasha did not put the pup out again, it lasted through the next day, but I had to keep attaching her to a teat where she did suckle, but she was still very weak and kept falling off the teat and had to be put back on and at times held there while she fed. I could look after her during the day, and make sure she got a regular feed, but being on my own I had already had very little sleep, and staying awake another night to make sure she fed herself all the night was a tall order. One that was just not possible in my state of exhaustion.

She died later during the following night.

Chapter Three

Left with the two boys things finally settled down to some kind of normality. Tasha would come down in the morning for her breakfast with the others. She would go outside for a penny and then back upstairs and feed her family. She insisted on being taken out for her walk, so was run down the road and back just to keep her happy. Sweep would not leave her pups but Tasha was not going to let her normal routine be interrupted for anything, the kids would just have to wait. It seemed to work because she then went back to her Mothering duties after her usual biscuit for going out; just getting her priorities right. I made sure I wiped her paws before I let her upstairs to the litter to make sure she did not take any infection up there. She still liked me to be around or else she would come and look for me, often with the litter screaming for Mum. So I had to take her back upstairs and settle her back into the whelping box. She was not the most attentive of Mothers but she did an adequate job.

Puppies do a lot of their developing after they are born. They are born blind and can only crawl in one direction, forwards. They only have senses at the end of their muzzle, this is so they can find the teat and suckle. I always weigh them every day when they are this small to make sure they are gaining weight or at the very least maintaining their weight. Now there is another story. Metrification. When I was at school we were going metric, in a few years the imperial system would be out, another result of the Common Market. So that was all we were taught, at the time. Years later we are still measuring things like speed in miles per hour and weighing in pounds and ounces. If you don't believe me take a look at the racing page in any daily paper, everything including the jockey's weight is in stones, pounds and ounces or furlongs and miles for distances. When I first obtained Sooty and Sweep I started to weigh them for some reason in pounds and ounces. Don't ask me why, and when my vet wanted to know their weight I had to convert it to kilos. When sweep first had pups I weighed them in kilos. Only on a routine visit to the vet she told me that she did puppies in pounds and ounces. What I wanted to know was at what point did she do the swap over?

Puppies' eyes open at around ten days, and you have to make sure that as this happens you do not expose them to bright lights for a few days until they are fully open, so flash photography is out. For this reason I use a very low wattage bulb in the bed room light. Their eyes start to open as slits and gradually get wider and wider until they are fully open, and the pup can now see the world around it for the first time. Although their vision is still not as good as an adult dogs will be. Their ears also start to open and they can begin to hear things also for the first time. So now is the time to introduce them to the sound of household appliances like the television, the radio and the vacuum cleaner. It is about now that they then start to want to get on their feet and move around. The gold progressed as normal with this and started to stand up, although a little wobbly for a start, but he was up in a fashion. This is where the Mother starts to get harassed because she can no longer leave them, they are now able to follow her, and there is no escaping them anymore.

His black brother though seemed to be having problems. I didn't take much notice at first because he could be a little bit of a slower developer than his sibling. But when his lack of progress continued alarm bells began to ring.

I spoke to the father's owners – sometimes talking to other breeders helps because they have either encountered a similar problem or know someone who has. They had no suggestions except a vet visit. So I took both of them, because that way they could see how far advanced the brother was. The vet we saw fetched her boss who bred dogs herself. She told me he was a swimmer and that his chances were not good. She suggested I could try to somehow manipulate his legs, but she really did not hold out a lot of hope for him.

I could not believe I was hearing this, and left in a near daze, barely able to take in what I had just been told. Not again. Another one that was not going to make it. So I was going to be left with the one pup. When I got home I phoned another breeder, who happened to be taking her cat to see their vet that evening, so she suggested I brought the pup along for a second opinion. She said she would speak to her vet so that they would be expecting us.

I was at this point in a kind of trance and in no state to argue. I had never asked for a second opinion before, I have not had any cause to, and it would not be something I would do in normal circumstances, because the only thing I have had to complain about with my vet is the size of the bills I get sometimes. So that evening I reluctantly put both pups in a box with a vet blanket and a hot water bottle underneath that to keep them warm as it was going to be a cold night, and headed for Boston and a lay-by near Asda where I had agreed to meet Lucy.

While I was waiting for Lucy to arrive, I sat there watching the world go by as normal, as people made their normal way home in their normal fashion and in their normal life routine. None of those going passed could know what was going on only feet from where they walked, laughing and joking with their mates as they, school children, shoppers workers and all, made their way home. This little puppy laying against his brother in a deep slumber was relying on one person and one person alone to fight his corner for him here, and that was me. It was getting dark very quickly as it does in the dead of winter, a cold moonlit night.

The pups were asleep on top of each other, huddled together for warmth, but they weren't cold, it was just a natural sleep heap as puppies do when they are very young. After about ten minutes a car drew up behind me and flashed its lights. It was Lucy. By now the sun had gone down some time ago and it was dark except for the silvery moonlight. Lucy pulled out and took the lead because I was not certain where we were heading. She pulled into a tiny car park under a bridge which went over the weir of the Witham that marked the barrier for the tidal flow, and I followed. With two estate cars there was hardly room, but we managed to get squeezed in.

It was very cold by now, with the light gone altogether the temperature was falling like a stone, so I took the pups out of the front seat where they had been travelling in their plastic box beside me, and whisked them into the surgery and the warmth. They were still sleeping. Oblivious to what was going on.

Lucy spoke to the receptionist and we sat down to wait. The wait seemed like it was taking forever. Like waiting for an execution. The lass sat next to me fell in love with the pups and said how nice they looked. If only she knew. I didn't go into details, I don't think I could. I was feeling sick as the whole situation felt as if it was just out of my control. I was being helplessly bowled along like a cork in a violent stormy sea of despair.

Eventually it was our turn and we were called in. Thomas started with Lucy's cat. I think he wanted to deal with the easy option first. And then it was my turn. I took them both out of the box and put them on the table. Arran started to sniff around in his usual inquisitive manner. I had to get him to stand up, but he obliged, to demonstrate how far advanced he was compared to his brother.

Thomas said the same as my vet, he was a classic swimmer. He was flat chested from being on his tummy all the time, like someone had taken him and flung him splat onto the floor, as bread makers do with dough. Thomas listened to his heart and confirmed that he also had a heart murmur. Because of his flat chest, there was not enough room in there for his heart to function properly. He said that by some miracle he may get on his feet and suggested putting him into some kind of channel to force his legs underneath him to try and get him to stand up, but he was not over optimistic about the success this would have. Lucy then asked him what he would have told her if it was one of her dogs. He said he would have told her to have it put to sleep, and that he had not said that to me straight away because he didn't know me. He also advised that the best thing would be to get it done sooner rather than later because the longer I left it the harder it would be. I could see the logic in this.

It didn't make the inevitable any easier though. When outside and putting them back into the car Lucy said that the fact he had a heart murmur would worry her.

With this ringing in my ears, along with everything else that I had been told today, about this little dog who had done nothing wrong, because so far fate had not given him the chance to as yet, I got into the car and drove home.

I don't know what I was expecting to come from this, I know what I was hoping for, I wanted someone to come along with a miracle cure and make everything okay again, but in the real world this was just not going to be. But then that is the difference between the two parallel universes of reality and fantasy. The reality was cruel and unforgiving. I did not sleep a wink that night tossing and turning all the time with Thomas's words going round and round in my head. I couldn't get it out of my mind, I also couldn't think straight. In the early hours I had made my mind up. If he wasn't going to be able to stand up and run around like a normal puppy, then it was not fair to let him go on. I would phone work in the morning to let them know I would not be in, and take him to the vet as soon as they were open. Get it over with.

When morning reluctantly came I got out of bed at the usual time. I didn't look inside the whelping box, I didn't want to because I could not face looking at them, and particularly the black pup. There were no sounds from in there, so everything must be okay. Tasha followed me downstairs and went out as usual with the others, came back in and had her breakfast before returning to her pups.

I had a quick breakfast which was difficult to eat and keep down, or at least I think I did, I may not have bothered, my mind was all over the place and certain irrelevant details have now become uncertain, a blur in a sea of harsh reality. What really mattered here was a life that was about to be extinguished forever. I took all the adults out for their walks just down the road as usual. When she got back, Tasha returned upstairs. Just as if all was as normal.

Except it wasn't. By half eight the pup would be dead and it would all be over. I knew for a fact that my vet would not argue with my decision in the circumstances.

At eight o'clock I drove the car out of the garage and went to close the door. I stood on the drive. Now all I had to do was go and get the pup.

But I couldn't do this.

Before I had chance to change my mind I ran up stairs, looked at Mum and pups, they were fine, got changed, and went to work. I don't think I have ever been so keen in my life to go to work. When I got there I went to my desk and sat down and cried. Julie sat opposite me said the most useless thing I have ever heard "Don't upset yourself." What else was I supposed to do? I was about to kill a new life. Having an old dog put to sleep when all else has failed at the end of its life is hard enough, but to do this to a pup that has not yet had a chance at life?

Impossible.

I somehow managed to get myself through the morning. Don't ask me how. I think I just tackled all those boring jobs that do not require any brain power and are normally left as long as possible, but right now anything that did not require much thinking was good. I was going to have to face the inevitable and have the puppy put to sleep. It was my duty as his owner to do the best thing for him. And no matter how many times I went over the possibilities it came down to the same conclusion, there were no other options. Easier said than done.

So it was with a heavy heart that I went home to lunch as usual to let them all out for a penny and check on the pups.

I had not been home long when the phone rang. Now who was this?

"Hello?"

"Its Mum, have you had that dog put down yet?"

"No."

A long pause followed before I dared to venture," Why?"

"Well Alan Rogers reckons there is a chance you can get him up on his feet if you work his legs for him"

I had to bite my fist here to stop myself bursting into tears. I bit it so hard it hurt and left teeth marks. But the pain and damage were irrelevant. At last I had someone with an answer, a glimmer of hope, a light at the end of what had been a very long and dark tunnel. I could have shouted the news from the rooftops. I nearly broke down in tears again as I replied "Well would he come and show me how?" trying to suppress my rising euphoria. I wanted to be sure there were no mistakes made here; so really needed someone who knew what they were doing to come and show me how to do this to make sure I was doing it correctly. A precious little life was depending on it, and there was going to be no second throw of the dice if this wasn't done right. This was to be his very last chance, and if anything went wrong I did not want to be thinking forever more "had I done this right?"

Alan was an old friend of my Dad's, and Dad had gone to see him because he had an old fridge freezer that had broken down and wanted to see if Alan wanted it to tinker around with. He didn't want it as it was, but he happened to ask my Dad how the pups were and Dad had told him about the swimmer and asked him whether it really was the end of the road for the little dog. Alan had said "No" because he used to breed Labradors for shooting dogs and had experience of one or two like it himself in the past, and had been successful with them. As he put it "they often make the better dogs."

My Dad brought Alan round that night and he took a look at the pup. He showed me how to work his front legs for him, if he got up on those, his back ones would follow he told me. I asked how long I should give him to improve. He said a week. Not that long for a dog that could not even clear the floor to be expected to be up and on his feet.

So straight to it; no time like the present. Every time I went into the bedroom, I worked his legs for him in a circular motion as I had been shown. Very gently because the bones are very soft at this age, I was only trying to tone the muscle. To give some rhythm and timing to it, I would work his legs to "round and round the garden like a teddy bear", and on the "one step ...two step" I would gently pull the legs apart to work the chest muscle. I would do this routine a couple of times on each visit and then place him back in the bed with his Mother and brother. Tasha did not seem to have any objections to my handling her pup, and he did not protest either.

It was a case of every time I went to the loo, work the dog's legs, go to the loo, wash my hands, back into the bedroom and work his legs again. Went up stairs for something, work the dogs legs. One time I sat during the first half of Coronation Street with him laid in the middle of my knee on his back, just gently working his back legs up and down, I know Alan had said his back legs would just follow as he got up on the front, but it would do no harm. He was fast asleep, very contented and totally out of it, and oblivious of what I was doing.

His progress was astounding, almost unbelievable in the least. You could see the improvement by the hour at the very start, let alone by the day. And as he began to show signs of standing up and moving around, his brother started to take a renewed interest in his sibling, whom up to now he had left alone, apart from putting his arm around him when they were laid together, as if to protect him. He had seemed to sense that his brother had something wrong. He now started to pull at him and wanted to make him move, and the black pup would take so much, and then took a swipe at his brother, and the gold would retreat to another corner of the box out of the way for a bit before returning later for another attempt at getting his brother to play.

Some had suggested that it may be an idea to separate them to give the black a chance. But I think the gold pulling him about a bit was giving him incentive to try and move, if only to give his brother a biff. Right or wrong, the result was good, it was getting him moving and using his legs.

But for the grace of God he would have been pushing up daisies. And thinking about it even now still brings tears to my eyes. If I had been able to face taking him to the vet that morning he would be dead. And had that fridge freezer not been broken my Dad may not have spoken to Alan. It doesn't bear contemplating all the "what ifs". If the pup does not believe in God then he should at least do so in guardian angels, because his was certainly watching over him that morning when fate was on his side.

Somewhere in all this mayhem I had even turned into a Chinese Acupuncturist which I happened to be passing, to see if they could help. A translator had to do all the interpreting between me and the practitioner, so what was said exactly I don't know, but it took a significant amount of time to stress that yes I was enquiring for a dog, you know, animal about so high head at one end tail at the other and a leg in each corner, the upshot was they didn't think they could help, but hey, it was worth a try.

Chapter Four

By the time the week was out he was up and on all fours. Shaky, but up and walking, or maybe a better description would be wobbling around, but best of all, beginning to play with his brother. There was no stopping him from here on. His legs were bowed to start with but slowly, very slowly they straightened as he quickly became steadier on his pins. His chest began to fill out properly, and he was looking more like any normal Cocker puppy should, and ready to be moved downstairs with the others and face the big wide world. With puppies, a puppy pen, like a toddler pen for very young children, is an absolute must. Adult dogs round your feet when trying to work in the kitchen or anywhere in the house are a pain, but puppies are smaller and can get in all the places the adults cannot reach. It also helps keep the puppies and the adults separated, particularly when feeding because all the adults will do is muscle in and pinch the pups food given half the chance. Especially when they have their fourth meal of the day, which the adults do not get. When Niki had pups I used to let her finish off whatever the pups left, which wasn't a great deal, but what I had not realised was the food being highly nutritious made her put on weight – fast, which is okay for puppies because that is what you want, but not for adults. It was not until I took her to a local show just to get her back into the routine of showing, that as I picked her up to put her on the table, I realised just how chubby she had become, purely by eating the puppies left overs. She had become that heavy the table nearly collapsed under her weight. I stopped letting her clean up the puppies food after that, and with a little extra exercise she was soon back in shape.

A pen is also useful just to be able to put them in there now and again out of the way, without having to be looking where they are all the time and at every step you take in case there is a pup under foot. Or be looking in all the hidey holes both past, present and in anticipation of future ones they may come up with, to find them, because just like with children, when they are not making a noise you begin to wonder what they are up to. The pen works perfectly until they are able to climb out, after that point there is no stopping them, and when they get to a certain size they can scale the sides like they are no longer there. Prince (Niki's brother) was particularly adept at escaping and Niki was often left in the pen on her own crying after her brother who was running around loose.

So now it came to needing names for the two of them. I don't like to decide on names or even think about possibilities too early, as I have done this in the past, and if the pup doesn't make it, it makes it harder to deal with the loss. For a whole fortnight the black pup was known as "Hotpoint", because it was one of their fridge freezers that had effectively saved his life. Another possibility for him was Lucky, but this was rejected because we'd had a previous dog called that. And although she had been dead a long time, and my parents also agreed that it would not bother them, it somehow did not seem right.

My Grandfather called all his dogs by the same name, when I asked why he did that, he said "Judy" just rolled off the tongue. When talking about a past dog the only way to distinguish which "Judy" you meant was by reference to the colour of the dog. When I was young he had a pure white mongrel and she was always referred to as the "white Judy". I liked dogs right from the start and looked forward to seeing her when I visited. And more than anything I wanted us to have a dog of our own, but as previously mentioned Ian did not like them. After the white Judy died I remember my Granddad getting her replacement. I went with him and my Dad to get the new dog, a mongrel of the same type, but this one was white with large black patches, she was thus referred to as the "black and white Judy". We went in my Dad's car because my Granddad could not drive. The bloke we bought her from wanted ten bob for her (fifty pence in new money). My Granddad as usual like the Queen was not carrying any money so my Dad actually paid for her, so technically she was his dog, because he never did get that ten bob back. The bloke's little lad stood at the farm gate with tears in his eyes when we drove off with her. I sat in the back with my arm round her all the way back. For some reason she would never go into the house and spent her whole life outside and in the kennel for her meals and sleeping. She had been kept outside up to now so why change?

It was my Nan who told me that dogs had better hearing than us, and I used to think she meant that they could hear things louder than us and not that it had anything to do with the range of sound they could hear, physics was not my strong point or something I was even aware of at the time. You have some real strange theories when young, and that seemed perfectly logical to me. She also told me that puppies came from underneath the gooseberry bush, which was also quite feasible because they had a whole load of said bushes in their front garden. You would not believe the explanation I got when I asked how you told the difference between a dog and a bitch. But I spent a lot of time trying to tell which was which "Just by looking at them"!

The gold pup I named Arran, after the Isle of Arran, to fall in with his Uncle, Tobermory. Toby got his name because one night the map fell open at that page, he wants to think himself lucky it did not fall open at another page, or heavens knows what name he would have ended up with, I dread to think. The black pup finished up with the name Jack, because when he was moved downstairs after weaning him, he used to sit in the corner of the kitchen, like Jack Horner, out of the way of all the others while waiting for his food to be prepared. I started to give him his meals in the cage because he was slower at eating than the rest of them and still very timid. The others would take full advantage of this if I did not watch them, and it was just easier to put him in a cage and shut him in there, then I did not have to concern myself about keeping five other dogs away from him until he had eaten all his food. He soon cottoned on that he had to eat faster and while he still eats in the cage the door now remains open. He usually finishes first anyway and goes on the hunt round all of the others bowls to see if he can get any extra. They all tell him the same thing, and he has the good sense to take heed of the warning growl he receives when he gets too close as he tries to approach any of them, and sensibly retreats to a respectful distance.

He will often use the cage as a retreat to be out of the way, and that is where he takes all his "treasures" for safe keeping, or so he believes. These include the inner tubes of kitchen rolls which he delights in pulling to pieces. If he can find one at bed time he will race upstairs with it and station himself under the bed and will not let anyone go near him. Arran, his brother, will sit in the cage at times but Jack does not like it and always checks that everything is as it should be when he comes out, and that nothing is missing. Toby will also sit in there last thing before bedtime, but Jack daren't say anything to him, but I am sure he doesn't like the idea of any other dog using what he sees as "his" cage.

Jack even objects to the weekly changing of the fleece blanket that is in there for him to lie on, and gets even more concerned when it disappears into the washing machine. He keeps all the hooves (the horn of a pig's trotter) in there as well, and Arran has got to sneaking in and taking one out down to a fine art, as he has never been caught yet.

Had he been a girl, Jack is the absolute spit of his great aunt Sooty, in both his appearance and his mannerisms. He has got that curly knot of hair on the top of his head which is not supposed to be there. So that is a weekly job with the thinning scissors to try and keep it under control. He will also look at me in a sideways manner out the top of his eyes, just like Sooty did, when I am telling him off.

Picking a puppy out is a skill, and if you are not very experienced on which of a litter are going to make the grade as a show dog, it is best left to someone who is, and a second, third, fourth etc opinion can always be useful. They will also need to be trusted to be impartial with their advice, so that could mean someone who is a judge of, but at the same time is not specifically owning and showing your breed, and then you are not going to be in competition with them in the show ring at any time in the future. Lucy breeds Golden Retrievers but has judged Cockers in the past. She said that Jack would not make a show dog, the best one was Arran. So the best thing to do with Jack was advertise him for sale. He had been to his vet for his first inoculation and I made a point of getting them to check his heart, but they said he was fine. So his heart murmur had gone as his chest had filled out properly, giving it the required room to function.

Every time we saw a different vet I would ask them the same question about his heart; although it was the best news since getting up onto his feet, I wanted to be absolutely certain he was going to be okay before he was offered for sale. There was one young lass who would take an age to examine the dog, so when she was taking surgery once when he went for something, I asked her to check him, and after what seemed like half an hour with her stethoscope pressed to different sides of his chest, she finally took the stethoscope out of her ears and confirmed he did not have a heart murmur. After that I was convinced, and stopped asking any more.

But even if he did still have a heart problem, at least he could now run around like any normal dog, and if one day whilst chasing a rabbit or something, he has a heart attack and dies, at least he will have had a shot at life. However his vet had passed him as A1 fit, which was an added bonus and meant he could confidently be offered for sale.

Fate took another twist here because he was on the Kennel Club website for three months, and was advertised in all the local papers. Several people made enquiries, but were not keen on the asking price. But he was not going for anything less just to get him sold. He was a pedigree animal with all the vet checks and inoculations.

I didn't take him to ring craft classes, because after all if he was going to be sold so there was no point. So when he didn't sell he was thrown in at the deep end. I took him to a local show just to see how he got on. He was really nervous and actually tried to snap at the judge, he probably thought he was at the vets and was going to get an injection which had been the case so far when he was stood on a table, especially in front of a female. Also being owned by a man it made him slightly nervous of women. Sweep was the same, she always responded better to male judges, and consequently did better under them. Fortunately for Jack the judge stuck with him and examined him all over. She could have quite rightly asked me to withdraw him, but she didn't, and for that I am most grateful. He wouldn't stand properly and didn't walk very well, as he was very nervous and kept looking all around him instead of concentrating on the job in hand. So there were no surprises when he didn't get placed anywhere, but the experience would not have done him any harm.

The idea behind ring craft classes is to get puppies used to showing before they are introduced to their first real show and they get familiar with being felt all over and walking round so that they are not "cold" when they first go into a ring. It is a good idea when they are young to get as many people as you can to touch the dog and get them used to being handled by different people. Some people use treats in an abundance to encourage the dog, particularly puppies, which can cause a problem for later classes, especially in rings that are on grass, any dropped treats remain there and the dogs in subsequent classes spend all their time with their noses to the ground looking for whatever they might be able to find. I particularly get this problem with Tasha, and this includes when she is supposed to be walking round in front of the judge with her head up. She sees the ring as a chance for an extra snack and will go round with her nose end down on the ground, sweeping her head from side to side, hunting for whatever she can find, and Jack is also cottoning on to this fast and does the same.

I don't bother with treats, I think there is enough clutter to hold in your hands with the dog lead and a brush, without fishing for a treat every two minutes.

The next time I tried taking Jack to a show he went on his own. His first open show was at Heckington. By only taking the one dog I would be able to give him my full attention and hopefully boost his confidence. Because it was a boiling hot day he sat in his cage underneath a Mediwrap blanket which is silvered on one side and is used by ambulance and rescue crews to keep a casualty warm, but used the other way round they can also deflect the heat. He was as cool as a cucumber under there. He sat there watching a train run up and down just behind his cage on one of those miniature railways which give rides to all the kids (and adults with the real little ones) and was quite content with that. Boy dogs do like doing "boys" things. With owning both dogs and bitches a difference in their behaviours and interests is noticeable. If I start doing any DIY or "man's" work, the boys want to get involved and will sit there and watch me, whilst the girls just go to sleep and totally ignore what I am doing. Jack and Toby are keen little tractor and train boys, and enjoy nothing better than watching a train go passed if they are at the front of a queue at a level crossing, or watching a tractor go up and down ploughing a field they happen to be walking passed. Toby as a puppy did not like motorcycles passing him in the car, if he spotted one out the back window coming towards us he would start to whine which would get ever louder as the motorcyclist approached and over took the car. Mind he was a good early warning system.

A trait that Jack has picked up straight from his great Nana Sweep is if he does not want to be bothered with showing that day I may as well pack up and go home and save myself some time and money, because just like her he will not walk properly if he is not in the mood.

However he must have been in the mood that day because he didn't do too badly, he was not last in his class and seemed more settled and much calmer about the whole thing. It was whilst walking round the show ground with him looking at all the stalls that someone stopped me and said what a lovely looking dog he was, and asked where I had got him from. I told them he was my own breeding and they wanted to know if he was still for sale. I said no, not anymore. He had stayed too long to move him on now, for any price, so this was not even discussed. He was staying.

The only snag with being a show dog is that your coat has to be in good order. This involves both trimming and brushing. Jack can be a real wuss when it comes to brushing him. He hates any knots in his coat being pulled with the slicker brush, and has perfected the art of shouting out well before he is hurt, because he knows it will make me stop. He does the same thing if I stand too close to him, he will yelp just in case I did stand on him regardless of whether I did or not. His brother is not keen on a brush either and will try a different tack of growling at me, that is if I have managed to catch him in the first place, because if he sees me coming or waiting for him he dives behind the sofa and won't come out until he thinks I have given up and gone away. That is when the long tail can come into its own as a last resort to catch him before he disappears completely. The other alternative is move the sofa.

Jack's brother Arran, the one who had been earmarked to be the show dog, had a problem. Only one of his testicles had descended. There were various theories from many quarters (as there always is from the know-it-all brigade) about how long I should give it to come down, which ranged anything from the moment he was born to eighteen months. There were also various rumours about a procedure to have a false one fitted. I never mentioned this to my vet because it was not even going to be considered. It is not an option in the UK anyway. If it wasn't down at eighteen months he would have to be castrated, no question, otherwise there was the possibility it could turn cancerous. At the end of the day his health and well-being came first. So at eighteen months that was the end of his show career, and something else that was probably very dear to him. Though despite his lack of tackle he did get a fifth prize from Spilsby show in a puppy class, the judge must have either forgiven him for only having one or else forgot to check. In fourteen years of going there that is the only time we have come away with a rosette. Companion Show results can be all over the place, one week your dog is flavour of the month and the next no one wants to know.

Sooty was no show dog either. She was too small and carried her tail wrong. She had what is known in some circles as the "Broomleaf back end." Something, which thankfully, has not continued down the line. The tail is set far too low down their back, almost like the dog is continually carrying it between the legs; as if they have done something they shouldn't and know it.

But despite not being a show dog, she still liked to go because she enjoyed being there and the taking part, she looked very down if she was left at my parents because to take both of them I needed someone with me to hold her whilst I took Sweep round, as being identical ages and sex, they were both in the same class. When she did go I think she was so pleased that I had taken her and got over excited at the prospect, which was not good, because she would just bound around everywhere including up and down the ring. But now and again a judge would take a shine to Sooty, and with her and Sweep being litter sisters they were deadly at brace, because they always walked out together all the time anyway. What they would do sometimes when moving round together is swap sides at about the half way mark, but unless the judge was looking specifically at them when they did it, they made their move so smoothly without breaking step, if you blinked you would miss it. This was okay if all the pairs were sent round together but if we were sent round one pair at a time, which some judges preferred to do, that made it impossible to conceal so I had to do my level best to stop them changing sides.

As table dogs they have to be lifted onto the table for the judge to first examine them and then lifted off again to be moved around the ring individually as requested, usually in a triangle so that the judge can see the dog moving from all sides. From behind as they walk away from the judge, from the side as they walk across from the judge on the second side of the triangle and finally from the front as they come back to the judge. Some will also move them straight up and down as well. Sooty did not like being picked up at the best of times unless she wanted to be, and would protest with a prolonged growl in her loudest possible voice. I could usually get her onto the table without too much protest, but she would growl and kick her back legs like a child having an issy fit, showing her displeasure at being lifted off. To stop her I found if I were to lift her ear flap and blow in it as I picked her up, the shock of the sudden rush of air took her totally by surprise and she promptly forgot all about her little tantrum.

Sweep on the other hand would have quite willingly opted out. If she was not in the mood then I may as well have stayed at home, so it is obvious where Jack gets it from. She would just slouch as she was walked round in the ring and show no interest in the proceedings at all. And catching her in the mood to coincide with a show was nigh impossible. A well timed shot from a bird scarer one afternoon did the trick and got her a prize in a show, because it went off just as the judge was looking over the class for one final time, and Sweep suddenly stood to attention looking all alert and ready to go, all she needed was someone to give her the command.

To Arran any kind of noise remotely like gunshot is all he needs to get excited about the prospect of the hunt, even if it is military artillery fire, and like all good gun dogs, the sound of gunshot gets his undivided attention. The bombing range on this particular occasion was being used by an army chinook helicopter and they were shooting artillery fire at targets. The fact that the shot had a totally different sound to a shotgun did not deter his enthusiasm as he tore off after the helicopter to help retrieve whatever they were shooting at. The fact that I still have him is testimony to the fact that I did manage to stop him before he got onto the range and ended up being shot.

Sweep, whilst in the ring waiting for her turn, would spend a lot of time taking an interest on what was going on in the ring next door, which nine times out of ten would be obedience, instead of concentrating on the matter in hand. It is a pity she did not pick up any tips and even if she did, at least try practicing them from time to time.

When Sooty and Sweep were both entered in the same class as individuals, someone else would handle Sooty. They would try to go to each other if they passed too close as the sister was being taken round the ring, and a bit of forward planning had to be made to keep as much distance between them as circumstances and space would allow, Sooty would come charging down the ring on the outward journey and walk back up the ring looking over her shoulder at her sister. They would greet each other with glee when they were finally reunited. As Sweep was often selected and Sooty was not, Sooty would leave the ring with great reluctance and would insist on waiting by the entrance for her sister.

In a show at Newark I had taken them both into the ring for the brace class, so they were on a brace lead which is Y shaped and allows you to attach two dogs to the one lead. While all the pairs were getting themselves into line, for reasons best only known to herself, Sweep decided to try and mount her sister. Not only did Sooty have a bit of a short fuse, but she did not do "that" except in the middle week of her season, and as it was not anywhere even near, she consequently turned on her sister. So there we were in the ring, two dogs that were supposed to be standing and moving together, knocking seven bells out of each other. They were really going for it and meant business. When I finally managed to separate them, they would not even look at each other and were doing their level best to stand as far apart as they could. The brace chain they were on was so taught that I could have played a tune on it. Remarkably, somehow, they still got a third, and no, money did not change hands.

Few dog fights between family members result in serious injury, it is usually a lot of spitting and swearing at each other but they hardly ever draw blood. Having said that Sooty and Sweep loved scrambled egg, particularly Sweep who would do anything if she knew that is what was in the offing. Once when I had prepared the three of them a bowl each, I put the bowls down as simultaneously as possible and they all tucked in to their respective helpings, so all was hunky-dory. So far. However, finishing hers first, Sweep decided to try and get extra off her sister, who promptly bit her on the ear in a last ditch attempt to save, what was rightfully, the remains of her egg which was quickly disappearing down her sister's throat, having already put an unheeded warning growl across Sweep's bows.

Sweep, undeterred by this, carried on eating the remainder of her sister's egg. Hearing the scuffle I turned to see blood spurting all over the place. There are a lot of capillaries in the ears for the blood to come from and by this time I had three dogs all with their heads together and no idea which one that it was coming from. So I had to separate them one by one, and sods law it was the last one I went to. After trying to stem the flow of blood with not too much success, I phoned the vet and the receptionist said she hadn't got a vet available as they were all out at lunch, but told me how to try to stop it by holding it in a paper towel really tight, and she stressed it would have to be really tight. Grabbing paper towel and locating the actual wound I did as I had been told and finally succeeded, after quite some time, in stopping it. That saved a few bob in vet's fees, although thinking about it, I have no idea how I was proposing to drive her, on my own, eight plus miles down the road with her ear bleeding, as I doubt bandaging would have been very successful.

I have also had five of them in a Family Group class, and because of the difficulty of handling five at once, I made it plain to the judge that there was no way I was going to move them. It was after getting them all set up and ready, that they decided to start scrapping between themselves, just as the judge was looking over all the entrants. Toby very kindly soon put a stop to it as my boss dog, and, miraculously, they got a first because as the judge put it, "It was just like a real family".

Sooty and Sweep were my first pair I entered in brace. When Niki came along she went in with her Mother Sweep, and Sooty became redundant, but by this time she was no longer so bothered about taking a back seat. On Tasha's arrival she was partnered with Niki, a welcome relief to Sweep as far as she was concerned. When Jack started to show I tried him with his Mother, but they did not normally walk together and they were terrible, and placed, quite deservedly, last on their first attempt. I vowed that was the last time I would enter that pair in a brace class. However they had both already been pre-entered in brace at the Norfolk and Norwich Show, held in conjunction with the Royal Norfolk Show. I was not going to give up the entry fee, my Lincolnshire breeding kicking in yet again, so we waited for the class to come up and took the plunge. While walking them round you need to be watching a) what they are doing and b) looking where you are going, so you cannot see just how well or conversely, badly, they are doing by your side, particularly with their back legs because these are actually behind you. We went round first, not the position I like them to be in, but we had just lined up that way. The dogs after us all walked perfectly, so that would be another last then. Anyway, the judge came across to us and asked me how old each of my dogs were, so I told him Tasha was four and Jack was one. He thanked me and walked off. He took a final look at all the entries before pulling mine out first. I could not believe it and went home that night on a definite high. It was a hot day and the brace class is often right at the end, so I had nearly come home on several occasions for the dogs sake, but I was pleased I had persevered. Ever since, it is very rarely they were placed any further back than a second, especially when Jack was the same height as his Mother, he has got a bit taller now, but there is not a great difference between them so they still score a first fairly regularly.

Navigating to some venues for the first time can be a headache, because if you are late and miss your class that is it, even if you have prepaid, time and tide and all that. The first time I went to The Royal Norfolk we arrived literally with minutes to spare as the traffic onto the show ground was unbelievable, so it was a case of a very quick tidy up with the brush for Sooty and Sweep and straight into the ring and down to business, at least they did not have time to get bored with waiting. On one such hunt for the venue I was driving around Newmarket trying to find the Rowley Mile course. There are two courses at Newmarket and I had already found the other one and had to find my way out of there, when I spotted an estate car with a dog guard and thought they must be going, so I followed them. Only they weren't, and ended up back in the town centre. There should be a law against driving a car with a dog guard near a dog show and not be going. One comforting statistic for all lost motorists out there, at any one given time – up to twenty five percent of drivers currently on the road are also lost. You are not alone. Sat Nav was not on the go yet.

Where the dog show is part of a larger county or country show you usually get a concessionary ticket per dog entered. So if I have entered two dogs and not wanting to waste anything I usually offer the free one to someone else. Sandra, a work colleague, liked to go to Heckington, she would get a look round the rest of the show for free. Getting the opportunity to look round is something you do not get much of a chance to do when you are showing because you have a dog or two to look after and get ready for the ring. Sandra had pestered and pestered to go to a show, so I let her go to a local show when Toby and Tasha were pups, and with them being in the same class I would need someone with me to hold and show him for me. She was late getting there and only just made it in time, she had got lost. It was one of those tiny villages, one street long! Toby in five seconds worked out that he had someone on the end of the lead that did not have a clue what they were doing and just took full advantage of the situation. He would not stand, walk or do anything she asked him to do. Debby, another colleague, went with me to another show, but because she knew how to handle dogs, he wasn't going to mess her around and even behaved far better for her than he ever did for me. He knows just how far he can push me, with a stranger he had to be on his best behaviour. Given the time he would probably have got her weighed up and acted accordingly, but as it was he dare do no other than behave.

Peter helped me with Sooty at Revesby Show once while I was handling her sister. Sooty also picking up on her new handler's inexperience, she would not stand up for him on his first request, so Peter, very politely, almost pleading with her, he asked her to "Please stand." Turning round towards her I barked "Stand!" which she did immediately without further question or resistance. I commented, much to the amusement of any other exhibitors in ear shot "You can tell that dog is not yours." That was a scorching hot day and to try and keep the dogs cool until their class came up, we had taken them under a nearby tree and were trying our level best to also keep an eye on where they were up to in the ring. Only we were not doing a very good job because we nearly missed the class altogether. After their class was over and with getting nowhere, we brought them home as it was just far too hot for us let alone for them with a woolly coat on. In those days I was not so well equipped to cope with the hot weather and keeping the dogs cool.

Back to Sandra, being the dizzy person she is, turned up at a show in high heels one time when everyone else was in wellies because the night before there had been enough rain to float an armada. She had to be lifted out of the mud on more than one occasion. I have also had to help her find her car before now because she parked it near a "pylon", of which there were three. So we had to walk up and down all the rows back from my car because she had arrived after me, until we found it, three rows of God knows how many cars later. I have never seen as many navy blue cars in one spot, something to be said for having a sky blue pink one! Now when she goes with me she goes in my car. Though I have lost a courtesy car before now, it was the same make as mine, but it did not have roof bars which is what I look for. Fortunately it was not too large a car park and I did have some idea which row it was in.

Dogs also need a lot of clutter with them to these events. Water bowls, two, if you are taking two dogs. Water, large container of; food if the show spans dinner time; cage or even two cages if you are taking three dogs. Toby likes to be in a cage on his own and one time I had to use one borrowed off my Mother at a show, and it was just a tad too small for him, as shelties are a little smaller, and he had to sit stooped while waiting for his class came up. As he did not have to wait long this did not matter too much, a cocker will adapt to anything you can throw at them and will just accept most situations, which is just as well sometimes.

Chapter Five

It is no use keeping a Cocker Spaniel and being house proud. When they go out for a walk they will gallop through all the mud in sight, and even find some that isn't just for good measure. Then they come home and don't bother to wipe their feet. Surprise surprise. The mud dries, they shake themselves and where does all the dust off them go? So if you like a neat and tidy house that is spotless, this is not the breed for you because they are mud lovers, water lovers and lovers of rolling in all things smelly given half the chance; another, very appropriate, name for the Cocker is Water Spaniel, because they see water they have to be in it. Drawn like bees to a honey pot. I have often thought I would like a garden pond preferably with fish, but have rejected the idea because it would just become a dog bath, and God only knows what would happen to any aquatic life, probably suffocate from lack of oxygen and clean water due to the mud levels.

On the subject of all things smelly, Sweep decided to have a roll in a fresh cow pat and cover herself from head to paw in it, the only clean parts on the whole dog were her eyes (she probably had them closed in pleasure), and the end of her nose. Serves me right for taking her for a walk in a field that had cows in it. This is not a good idea because for some reason, other than the one just mentioned, the two do not get on and cows will chase after dogs. So there was nowhere clean on the whole dog to give her a light smack to try and show my displeasure. Twenty minutes later when I got her home, (fortunately we were walking so I did not have to ride home with her in the car), I was still chuntering at her and made her wait out in the yard while I went up stairs and filled the bath. I should have hosed her down out there where she was, but I don't think I had a hose pipe at the time, but probably purchased one as a matter of priority soon after. It was a long way up those stairs to the bath room with one smelly dog right under my nose. There is something to be said for a down stairs bathroom, despite what the property experts may tell you, they obviously do not keep a dog.

The smell of fish is by far the worst thing they can find to roll in. A fisherman leaves a fish on the bank side and when it is half rotten and really smelly is when the dog is most attracted to it. And try to get rid of the smell. Bathing does sweeten the dog up, but you can smell it in the house for days. I don't care what the adverts on the TV say, those air fresheners, even the ones that huff and puff as you walk past, cannot combat this smell. Spray air fresheners are out because Niki is allergic to them. Take it from me this is the worst smell on the planet, and absolutely impossible to shift. Toby rolled in a fish once, when he got back in the car he sat one side of the boot and the others pressed themselves as far away from him as possible at the other, a bad case of BO even with all the windows open.

Bath time can be fun. They do not object too much to being bathed but they don't volunteer themselves either. Catching a particular dog can be both time consuming and an art. When I start to bath all of them it is a case of the first one I come to, but as I work my way through them my choices from the remaining number continues to deplete, and the last one is usually the least keen anyway. However, once in the water they will stand in the bath and let you soak and shampoo, then condition and rinse them. I have to shut the bathroom door before lifting them out, otherwise they would be off and dry themselves as best they know how in or on whatever comes to hand (or paw). This could include a dust bath, which with the wet coat would quickly become a mud bath, and all my hard work would be wasted. So I have to towel them off as best I can, then let them finish themselves off against any convenient object, keeping them indoors and away from anything that is likely to stick to wet fur; the way they go on you would think I had tried to drown them. (I will admit there are times when I could be tempted). All the old bath towels are saved to use for the dog because it takes two of these per dog bathed to dry them, and if I do all five in one day I have a pile of dog towels to wash, which quickly fills the washing line when they are all pegged out, so a sunny day is desirable just to get all the washing dried. Another reason for needing a warm sunny day is black dogs, as I have already mentioned, hold water like a sponge and they take the longest to dry. Sometimes though in an emergency where the dog has to be bathed, there is no choice on the weather conditions.

Such a case was when Toby managed to get himself stuck down a very steep sided gully on the bombing range. It happened on New Year's morning. You are allowed on the marsh when the RAF are not using it for target practice, and red flags are hoisted up and down to act as a warning to tell you when it is safe, as war starts on Monday morning at 9am and finishes at 5pm on the Friday night – weekends and Bank Holidays allow safe access to the bank top and marsh beyond. There is a two tier bank system here and you can walk on the top bank or the road that vehicles use just below, depending on how cold the wind is and from which direction it is coming, because the lower bank will offer some respite from what is a lazy wind that will blow straight through you rather than bother to go round, and there is nothing between you and Siberia out here, it is the usual first stop for migrating geese from Russia. In summer the breeze can be welcome, but not in the mid winter gales. The dogs do go over the upper bank and onto the marsh, but as a rule do not stray too far before I call them back. However this particular morning Toby had gone over the bank and out of sight which he often did and usually reappeared shortly after. When he didn't reappear given his normal time scale I called him a couple of times, still no sight or sound of him. I went up onto the top bank to look for him. Still no sign. I called "Toby" again. Still no dog. Fortunately I could just hear a whimper coming from somewhere out on the marsh. I went down the other side of the bank towards the sound to investigate, as I still couldn't see him and with that wind whistling about my ears I could hardly hear him. I followed his sound across the marsh. I had to keep calling to him to make him whimper. It was not until I was standing on the top of the gully that he had fallen head first into that I could see him. I could see how he had fallen in because it was just not visible, one more step and I would have joined him.

I had to haul him out using his collar. It was obvious by where all the mud was on him that he had fallen in head first, so the drop must have taken him by surprise like it nearly did me. Fortunately he had not broken anything; he looked okay anyway, which on New Year's morning could have been pricey if I had needed his vet. He was a bit shaken, but okay. He needed a bath when he got home. So I had to keep him in for an hour as it was bitterly cold in that wind outside; I turned the central heating up for him until he had dried off a bit. Fortunately for him he does not have a very thick coat and dries fairly quickly. I know I spend most of my time telling the dog to be quiet when he barks, but here is a good reason to teach him to bark on command. This is easily achieved by finding stimuli which makes the dog bark, telling him to bark just before the stimuli is activated and giving him a treat as he obliges. He will soon get the idea, and it may save his life one day.

Spaniel's ears, those endearing things either side of their heads that flap up and down as they run along and set their faces off to make them look so cute especially when you are trying to tell them off and that make you melt and give in when they are asking for something. The length of these appendages also causes problems. Not only when bathing them do you have to be careful not to get any water down them, but they also dibble them in everything they put their heads down to. This includes their food and water. You need special conical shaped water bowls so that their ears drape either side of the bowl whilst they drink, that is the theory anyway, and most of the time they do work. You can use a dolly peg whilst they are feeding to pin their ears above their heads if you are feeding them a sloppy meal. Or if you are feeling really flush you can get what are called "snoods" for them. You tuck their ears into these, and surprisingly they take to them quite well. These can also be used to keep grass seeds out of ears during the summer months. The number of those I have had removed over the years. In one particular summer I was thinking of asking my vet for her bank details so I could just have my wages paid straight into her account, and she could just let me have the change at the month end.

Just to be different, Sweep as a puppy, managed to get a seed up her nose one Sunday morning. I was just going to her to help, when she snorted it up her nostril, just as I was going to take hold of it. I was literally two millimetres away from taking hold of it. When we got home I phoned the vet who told me that she would most likely get it out herself, but if not she would need an operation to remove it. Likely story, more like he was not interested in a Sunday morning call out. It didn't come out on its own, she spent the night sneezing and rubbing her nose on the floor trying to get rid of the irritation. Next morning I took her to the vet without an appointment. They kept her in and sedated her to remove the seed. I was able to tell them which nostril to look in as I had watched it go up there. She did the self same thing years later, this time it was a decent day of the week although it was about seven o'clock at night, but you can't have everything your own way, and there was still a vet at the surgery, so I didn't have to feel guilty about calling her out.

Sweep also developed a problem with firework noise. Guy Fawkes has been dead now for over four hundred years and still the bloke is causing problems. There was a time of day that you could only let fireworks off on the night of November the fifth. The only concession to this was if the fifth fell on a Sunday because no one would dare to let them off on the Sabbath. Now they are let off on any night from when the clocks go back right through to the New Year. If you have a dog that does not like them, this can be a nightmare. Sweep was alright with them and did not take a lot of notice at first, after all, the last thing you need is a gundog who doesn't like bangs, and as I have already said a well timed gunshot is what was needed sometimes to make her pay attention. That is until the couple over the fence let one off right beside the fence just as she was stood on the other side of it. After that she hated the whooshing and screeching sound some of them make. In those early days there were not the calming drugs available that there are now. Putting the television on to try and drown out the noise is okay, but what is on the TV? Especially the soaps - you guessed - fireworks.

I bought her a CD with firework sounds on, and the idea was that I played it to her every night at a very low volume to begin with, when she was sat calm and relaxed, and over time increase the volume until it was such that it was played quite loud; and by this time the dog would be used to the sound and take no notice of it. But they are not an instant fix; I had to start using it months ahead of firework season. But it was some help, although she still disliked the screeching sound some of them made. The best thing is to stay calm and not make a great deal of fuss of the dog; else you only reinforce the fear. None of the dogs were allowed to sleep on my bed. The only concession was firework week. Sweep settled better if she was allowed on the bed beside me. She was not the best of sleeping partners because every two minutes she would itch something, then she would bite at something, then turn round, then another scratch, turn again. "For goodness sake either lay still or get off!" She would let out a long sigh and finally settle down. During the night when the fireworks had stopped she would get off and climb into the basket with Sooty. Although Sooty used to bully Sweep, I usually found them asleep together first thing in the morning, one usually with her head propped on the other one's back. She settled better to fireworks after we had moved. To begin with, there were not so many people letting the things off, and with the new location she did not connect the noise with her previous fear.

Although this breed has its problems, they do have a plus side. In their defence they are a very loyal, loving and intelligent companion. A busy breed, you just have to be prepared to overlook their apparent lack of understanding in obedience, and accept them for what they are. A dog bursting with oodles of love and character. Welcome to the world of the mad bad cocker. They will listen when it suits. Their understanding of the English Language appears to be intermittent according to the situation and circumstances. They will hear their own names if there is half a chance of anything food being available, or when they have nothing else better to do, otherwise – no chance. The words "Come here" when out for walks are just ignored as standard. Along with heel, sit, and stay. A self willed Cocker in obedience would be like trying to convert the Pope. It would be easier to get Royal Ascent than to get an otherwise occupied Cocker to do want you want him to do. A Cocker on a shoot working the field next but one to the one his now distraught owner, who has by this time nearly given up all hope of getting the dog to do as he is told, ie come back, is not an unusual sight. They need to be corrected firmly but also with kindness. If called and the dog does not respond, do not call him again, go and fetch him and lead him gently by the collar and bring him back to the spot you wanted him to come to in the first place. If you keep calling and calling this only encourages the dog to be disobedient. He needs to be taught that when you speak he reacts. Cockers unless kept occupied will very quickly go self employed.

The Cocker Spaniel is a very resourceful animal that will take full advantage of every situation presented to them and they apply a cunning canine logic to everything, and are always at least a step and a half in front of you at all times. Drop your guard and they will latch onto the opportunity with all four paws. They may not be on a par with the Border Collie but they are not stupid either. Niki just after we had moved had worked out where the box of Bonio was kept. And after I had left for work she had moved the pedal bin and pulled the box out so she could have access to it. How much help she got from Sooty and Sweep I will never know, but judging by the upset stomachs all three had, none of them were backward at coming forward to help her eat the whole box, and we are talking about a ten kilo box that had only just been started here.

Another example of their logical thinking is Tasha has worked out that those plums on the tree are edible and how to pull them. To begin with she would pull any she could reach, but soon learnt that they had to be a certain colour, and she will also sniff them, so is maybe using her powers of smell to detect if they are ripe or not. It did not take the others long to cotton on to what she was doing and copy her, so now she has competition. Particularly her son Jack who will start on the Czar plum tree as soon as they begin to turn colour. They have also learnt the same with the apples, but they only go for the eaters, the cooking apples are left to the birds. Arran is the only one that can reach the bird's nut holder which hangs from the washing line, he cannot get any out, but that doesn't deter him from having a try every now and again. Arran seems to have that extra reach that even Toby has not got. Arran can take things off the edge of the worktops in the kitchen and often will if he gets half a chance, so I have to watch what is near the edge or risk losing it.

Our first dog, Lucky, would wait behind the dustbin for the paperboy every morning as soon as she discovered he did not like dogs and that she could scare the living daylights out of him by lying in wait and jumping out at him just as he came round the corner. Someone had to go out every morning and rescue him and the paper because he would not come by her to the letter box. He used to wait just out of reach of her allowed by the chain that she was on, that is until the morning her collar broke, that moved him.

She also took great delight waiting for the Corona man every Monday morning, Bank Holidays would cause her confusion though, and it was usually well into the afternoon before she gave up her vigil. She would sit outside even in the rain waiting for him to come, and in the winter she would nip in for five minutes at a time to get warm and then go out again to continue her watch. She also liked to bark at the milkman, but he came a lot earlier and she was often still in the kennel, but this did not stop her letting him know she was there. She lost her bark once as the plumber that was called in for something kept her busy as he went in and out. For the best part of a week all she could manage was a hoarse woof which was hardly audible.

Dogs are very good at protecting what they see as their territory from any strangers and that can include the opposite side of the street if they can see it. My Nan used to leave the one door key they had hanging in Judy's kennel. It was going to be one brave burglar that was going to try to get hold of that. And anyway he would be instantly identifiable in any police line up by his lack of limbs. Lucky looked after our house key as it hung on a nail just inside her kennel door, before she came it was hidden underneath a child's bucket in the outside privy. Nearly as bad as under the flower pot, but I can just remember a time when the door was left unlocked if we were only going down the road to the shop.

The youngsters soon cotton on to what they have to do to be let out into the garden. During the long hot summer days the doors are always open, and they come and go as they please. But as the nights draw in and get chillier the door is not going to be left open all the time, especially with the heating running. Pups very quickly learn to do what the adults do and why they are doing it. But they all have a different way of asking to be let out. Toby will go to the door and if I am not concentrating on him he soon comes and gives me a nudge. Similarly to be let back in they will all sit and wait by the door looking in. Niki, however, will wait so long and then she will start to bark, and carry on barking until she is let in. Toby will, likewise, wait so long and then he will "knock" (he will scratch at the door), and like his Mum will not give up until I let him in. The others will just sit there and wait, looking in expectantly. I have not tested to see how long they would wait, or what they would do if left for too long. Tasha did get left out once. I had put them all out last thing before going to bed, and as they came back I counted them all in, or so I thought. In my defence at the time there were five all blacks and I did have a migraine. I was pleased to eventually get into bed, and did not, I will guiltily admit, do a final head count before getting into bed. Although it was early I went to sleep as soon as my head touched the pillow. It was about half one in the morning that I was woken and could hear a dog barking. I lay there thinking, "Will that dog be quiet!" After a few minutes it dawned on me that I recognised that bark. I switched the light on and had a quick count of dogs bodies laid in their favourite places round the bedroom floor, I realised I was one short, poor Tasha! Fortunately it was not a cold night, but she was still glad to be let back in, and I felt terribly guilty. Arran is lucky, because being a different colour to the other four; he is conspicuous by both his presence and his absence. Or maybe he would not agree, especially when he is doing something he shouldn't.

A sixth sense is a must when you own a dog. Eyes in the back of your head, and any other weapon of defence against this cunning logic. Mothers with children will already be half way there, because my Mum always seemed to know what I was doing without even looking, and I still to this day wonder how she did that. I think I am beginning to understand because if I hear one of the dogs doing something I have a good idea without looking which one it is and who to shout at. It is certainly a battle of wills. Sweep would keep picking all sorts of things up when out for a walk. So when she had hold of something she knew full well I would not let her have, she would walk just in front of me as good as gold keeping her muzzle hidden from me. I could tell that she had got something just by the way she suddenly started to walk those couple of steps in front of me. Niki would just hang back and hope I didn't look round and catch her. Tasha also tries the walking just in front and keeping her muzzle hidden. They have the intelligence to watch each other and copy the best ideas that seem to work for others in the group. That is why I do not like Arran going out with Toby for a walk, because Arran will copy him and Toby has all the bad habits imaginable. And quite by accident I have found that Arran and Toby will behave better if they are walked separately from each other.

Some dogs will sit and watch the television. Sweep would sit and watch "One Man and His Dog" all the way through if the whistling caught her attention at the start. Toby sat in front of the TV watching the whole first half of a womens football match, I think the ref's whistle was what caught his attention and he would not be moved for the whole of the first half, despite it being walk time, the rest of us had to wait for half time to come round when he lost all interest so was obviously indifferent about the final score. A theory since the advent of the digital TV is that dogs have become addicts because they can now see the picture, I do not agree with this because Sweep and Toby were not sat looking at just a series of dots with the analogue signal. Jack uses the television as a guide to tell him when it is supper time. He will sit watching for the titles and listening for the signature tune. I know he is using this as a guide because if I tape something that finishes at his feeding time and play it back at a different time of day, he will jump up in the hope that it is feeding time.

My Grandfather took his dog Judy to a furniture sale and while she was waiting with him, she caught sight of herself in a wardrobe mirror. Thinking it was another dog, she started to bark at it. He had to bring her out and tried taking her in again after a couple of minutes thinking she would have forgotten all about it. No chance. That did no good, as soon as she got back in she now knew where that dog was and what is more it was still there. The auctioneer asked him to leave, which Ted wasn't best pleased about because there was something coming up he had specifically gone for. Still no one had told Judy it was her own reflection and in her defence up to that point she had never seen herself. As far as she was concerned it was another dog. Niki did not like other black dogs; maybe she should have tried looking in a mirror. When I did try to show her her own reflection in the bathroom mirror and get her to wave her paw at herself, she would not even look at her reflection.

When out for a walk along the river side, Sooty liked to move any ducks sitting on the bank into the water as if she believed in the saying "a place for everything and everything in its place". And ducks should be on the water. One morning I had taken them into town for a walk along the river side and coming across a safe of ducks and on cue she moved them as usual, they flew across the river onto the opposite bank out of her way. Further up the bank we crossed over a footbridge and came back down the other side. When she got back to the same ducks, true to form, she moved them again. I don't know if ducks can swear, but judging by the louder quacking this time round, I guess it was not the politest duck speak as they flew back to the other side. Sweep would only chase something when she thought she had half a chance of catching it, otherwise she would not bother to waste her energy.

Sooty had a bit of a mishap with another paddling of ducks when she was really young. She was leaning over the bank edge looking at them on the water, her sister coming up the rear put a spurt on to see what her sister was looking at and misjudging her stopping distance knocked into her sister on arrival and Sooty went head first into the water. She was too small to get out on her own because the bank was quite high so she had to be lifted out by her collar. Ever since that incident she has never volunteered to get into a river again, but it didn't dampen her enthusiasm for chasing ducks.

She also had a habit when out for a walk of putting her nose into every mouse or whatever hole she came across and having a good sniff at the air inside. This was okay, but if the occupier was just coming out at the time she was going to get it bitten. She never did, which was probably down to sheer luck. Our first dog Lucky killed a little vole that came hurtling out of its hole without looking, saw Lucky and squeaked before turning round to go back inside. Too late; Lucky had bitten it and killed it, this all happened in the blink of an eye so I did not have a chance to stop her.

Sweep liked to spend a penny on all the mole hills she came across, and she had to be stood, often precariously, on the top of said hill to do it. Maybe it is a blessing she was a bitch and not a dog as standing up there and then trying to balance on three legs might have just been the tipping point, literally, especially if there was a strong side wind blowing. Dogs, as in the male of the species, seem to be content with standing at the side to do the business. The size of some of those molehills was nearly frightening. Sweep could stand behind some of them and be totally out of sight, I would have hated to meet the mole that made it face to face!

Sooty was an enthusiastic little dog who would walk forever, when we took a wrong turning in Sherwood Forest once, three hours later she was just getting into her second wind, whilst myself and Sweep were about bushed. Cockers are not deterred by bad weather either, they went out for a walk even if it was raining and no matter how hard. Fortunately just round the corner would settle them as long as they had been. If you want a rain shy dog this is not the breed for you. I would love a rain shy dog. My Grandfather had one, he would be going out shooting on his bike with Judy trotting along beside him (this was no doubt as illegal then as it would be today, but there was nowhere near the levels of traffic we have today, and he kept her to the back roads when she was running alongside), and if it started to rain while she was still close enough to home to find her own way back, she would turn round, come back and get herself into the kennel out of the wet and leave him to it. There was nothing she liked more than a shooting trip, but she liked the rain even less.

And the rain usually strikes when you are miles from the car or any other shelter. Walking along you can see the clouds gathering and convince yourself that they are not heading your way. And when it does become apparent that no, they are not going to go round you, it is too late. I have been soaked to the skin on more than one occasion, and the dogs look at you as if to say "what did you do that for?". Naturally it was my fault. A large towel permanently in the car is a must, because once a Cocker is wet that's it, it's like they never dry out. This is particularly true of blacks, reds and gold's are not as bad as they seem to dry out quicker because their coats are not as profuse.

No exercise. The worst news ever, especially if you are a dog, and certainly for the Cocker. They live to go for a walk. But it can happen for various reasons. Niki went to the vet because she was suddenly unable to stand on one of her rear legs, the vet confirmed it was not broken, so he gave her a week's worth of pain killers and said strictly no exercise and he would see her again when she had finished the course of tablets. She was not too bothered about the no exercise for the week and did not seem to be too put out when the others went out and she was left behind. I was told the same when Tasha had been spayed. Now this was a little harder to deal with; because she does live to go for a walk, just the same as her aunt Sooty did. She had to make do with just down the road on a lead for ten days. She was not supposed to be doing that, but she had to go somewhere to try and satisfy her. She just about coped, but she was like a coiled spring when finally given the all clear. There was no stopping her when she was taken out in the car and let out of the boot with nothing between her and her freedom.

Jack did something, not sure what, but all of a sudden he could not stand on his hind legs to reach up, not without it causing him to yelp and drop down again. I had no idea what he had done because I had not seen him do it which is often the case with dogs, so I was unable to give his vet any clues. She agreed he had not broken anything either, but Jack was still not happy at standing upright on his hind legs. After bending his legs this way and that his vet decided to give him some pain killers, and said to go back if he was no better by the time he had finished them, and she would have to investigate further and possibly x-ray him. And again the news was not good, no exercise.

I had an animal osteopath take a look at him, because he is my show dog and I needed him to be able to walk properly. She found a couple of things wrong with him, but it did not help his current problem. She thought he could well have a hair-line crack in his pelvis. When he had finished his pain killers, he was starting to improve, but he was still not right. I did not see the point in taking him to the vet again for them to x-ray him because if it was as suspected, a possible hair-line fracture of the pelvis, they would not be able to do anything anyway, it would just have to knit on its own. Which, if that is what it was, it did in its own time, because he soon returned to been able to stand up and jump around like he used to. At last, I had my old Jack back.

When puppies see snow for the first time they are uncertain what to make of it at first, approaching it with great caution, they sniff at it and lift their feet up one by one to begin with because it is cold to the touch. Sooty and Sweep experienced it in their first year when they were only six months old and struggled to get through some of the drifted parts that had piled up, but they did so in typical Cocker style valiantly battling on in the face of adversity. They played happily in the back garden burying their noses into it and running and skipping about for hours.

Jack and Arran did not see snow in their first year because that was a fairly mild winter. Around the wash area we don't seem to get the drifts the rest of the country get. There is the rest of Britain at a standstill and we are still moving. Although the attitude towards snow has changed since I was small. We went to school no matter what. I remember just after I had first started being amazed that you still went when it was raining. These days it only has to talk of snow and the education system grinds to a halt.

Jack and his brother were one year old before they experienced their first snow fall, and went out with the expected caution which soon evaporated as they followed the adults example and went bowling down the garden gleefully investigating this new phenomenon. They pushed their noses into the fluffy white stuff that was not there yesterday, sniffing and hunting for the grass which was somewhere around here when they last looked, but has now been covered with this wonderful material that may be cold to your paws but you can have such fun in, running around with your nose covered in the stuff hunting for all the hidden smells beneath here which still remain, but now need to be searched for by digging and rooting with your nose to find them first. Even looking for a place to do a penny has a new take on it and playing with your brother while the adults look on probably thinking "kids!".

There is a down side to this wonderful new white stuff, it sticks to the lacing on your legs, tummy ears and in between your pads, and forms hard ice balls which after time get so big because these clumps get ever bigger the more you walk in the snow, until you have to start swinging your legs in order to walk and after so long it gets so bad that you have to stop and wait for your owner to assist and try to get them off for you. I have had to smash these ice lumps between the handles of their extending leads because they get so compacted, this is the only way to break them up and get them off their fur. Sooty was a real wuss with this and would not go far before she wanted the ice removing. She also hated twigs in her under carriage and would not go a step further until it had been located and removed. (Not a very good gun dog trait if she did that every time on a shoot). Niki, now she is getting older, is becoming less keen on snow, just like the rest of us as time marches on.

Chapter Six

With Jack and his earlier problem it was some time before I dare to take him for a long walk, because puppies can be over exercised and this goes for up until they are twelve months of age as their bones are still developing, and they are still soft and it is possible to cause problems for later in life with too much exercise now, and in the case of a cocker they can still grow between the ages of one and two years. They need exercise but in moderation and do not need to be doing any marathon distances at this stage.

Anyhow he was on his feet, and with his first inoculation under his belt, there was going to be no stopping him now. After his second injection he was all ready to go. And a few days later I took him out with his brother and nana Niki for the first time. With pups I tend to take them out for their first few walks with their grandma so that they have a confident dog and a dog they know to follow along behind in the big wide world they suddenly find themselves in, although the inquisitive little mites do not stay behind the older dog for long as their confidence grows. Niki is very good for this because she will walk according to who she has got with her. She used to walk with her Mother in her later years and just used to amble along at Sweep's pace, guiding her along from her blind side. Then she would go out again for a proper walk at the usual top speed with her daughter.

To begin with Jack was not keen on being taken out in the car with the others, he preferred to stay at home with his great nana Sweep, who only went out in the car on rare occasions these days. But why should he, every time he went in that thing he ended up at vets and that resulted in a nasty jab in his neck. He was also travel sick, even on the shortest trips.

Travel sickness pills for dogs are available from the vets, although the herbal ones you can get off the shelf also do the job. But I am not a fan of pills for anything if there is a possible alternative to try first.

What I did with him was put him in the car and just took him round the corner to a nearby playing field. He then came round to the idea that car travel did have a happy ending, in this case an exciting walk with all new smells to investigate, and because the journey was really short he did not have time to even think about getting travel sick. Within a week he was asking to go with the others, and by gradually taking him further and further each time, he was soon able to travel as far as I would want him to go and actually looked forward to it, and all without a pill in sight.

Sooty was another dog that had problems with car travel to begin with. We found this out to our cost when I had talked my Dad into taking us all to see Mrs Cannelll. I did not have a car at that point and consequently the only car travel they had under their belts was the journey home when they were purchased and the short drive to and from the vets to get their inoculations done. It was admittedly a warm afternoon, but not that hot that it should cause any problems, I have subsequently taken dogs out in a car on far warmer days with no problems, and anyway arrangements had been made with both Mrs Cannelll and my Dad. I also did not want to disappoint Kathleen as she was no doubt looking forward to seeing her babies again. We set out and managed to get about half way there before Sooty was sick for the first time. Our line of thinking then was that after she had been sick and had an empty stomach, she should be okay from there on; this was not to be. We managed to get about another mile before she was sick again. We decided at this point to give up and turn back for home, and unless we stopped every half hour on the way back she would be sick right on cue, like she was sat there with a stop watch. When we got her home I phoned Mrs Cannelll to say unfortunately we would not be coming after all because we had to bring Sooty back and explained what the problem was. While I am sure she understood, and would not have wanted us to put her through any more trauma with travelling any further, I am also sure she was disappointed she would not be seeing her babies after all. Because as you get older, it is the little things that become ever more important.

I had up to the point of Sooty and Sweep's arrival resisted the ownership of a car. Quite content to tear around on a racing cycle on distances of up to ninety miles, you could keep your gas guzzling cars and all those expenses that go with them. But you can't take two dogs with you on a bike. Although my Grandfather used to take Judy shooting with him riding her on the front carrier of his bike. She would just sit there looking at the scenery going by, until she spotted a rabbit or other suitable chase-able subject, and then Judy went one way and Granddad went the other as he came off the bike because of the force of her launching herself into orbit after whatever.

Knowing about Sooty's travel problems, I would have to introduce her to car travel as sympathetically as possible. After talking to several people for ideas, I cured her with Stugeron tablets from the chemist, a herbal remedy for humans. The idea was to get her out without been sick and then she would not be thinking that just because she was in the car, she was going to be ill, which had been the case up to now. Sweep coped happily enough providing I stopped somewhere about every hour to let her get out to have a little run round to stretch her legs and for a few minutes breather. Sooty would always like to keep standing up using the dog guard and seat back as a support while she had a look round to see where she was going. Sweep on the other hand never appeared from when she was put in there to arrival. But she always seemed to know when she had arrived and where she had been taken to.

Sweep very quickly got into the habit of only reluctantly going out in the car, and I usually had to go and find and retrieve her from wherever she had chosen to hide. She always seemed to be happy enough when she actually got on the move and went quite happily for a walk when she got to wherever. She was not keen on going to dog shows, and quickly learnt that going out in the car meant there was a chance that that was where she might possibly be going, so just in case she would take evasive action. She was also reluctant to get back into the car to come home and would stop so far from it and sit or lay down and not come any further unless I went to fetch her and carry her to the vehicle. One time she did this when we came back from a walk in a wood. Sooty climbed into the car boot quite happily, she was always willing to go wherever. So to try and cure Sweep, as right on cue she lay down back up the track, and as we were on a quiet country lane I tried closing the boot, and me and Sooty drove off down the road a little way, pretending to go without her. I stopped a short distance down the lane to see what would happen now, expecting Sweep to come hurtling out of the gateway we had been parked in to see where we had gone. No such luck. When she still failed to appear, I reluctantly gave in and reversed slowly back again to see where she was. She was still where we had left her, she had not moved a muscle, seemingly not in the least concerned that she had been left behind. Either she really did not care or else she knew me better than I thought she did.

Travel sickness seemed to carry on down the line. Tasha and Toby were the worst to cure. Niki and Arran just didn't bother, too much like hard work for two dogs that are so laid back they are nearly horizontal. Now Tasha's problem is that she is no sooner in the car and just like a child with "Are we nearly there yet?" she starts crying because she wants to get out and get on with the walk. She was born light years too early; she is in desperate need of someone to invent teleportation. Any scientists on the verge of a break-through in this area and preferably with a prototype, please let me know, I have one very willing guinea pig for you.

The purchase of a car now meant I could take the dogs on holiday. If you want to take the dog with you the location you want to stay at and the one you can find that will accept your canine companion as well as yourself are very often a compromise. Although I think the tourism industry is coming round to the line of thinking that the dog is part of the family and if they want to make money then they have to move with the times.

"Dogs are not allowed on the furniture or in the bedrooms." Yes, try telling that to two dogs who considered both as a democratic right. So I took some old bed sheets with us and used them like dust sheets to cover all the chairs, and made sure that the cottage we were staying at had a hoover to clean up all the hairs they were going to deposit in a week. Another commonly used line is "Well behaved dogs only." Right, okay, as I look at my two. But in fairness to these two they do tend to pick up on when they need to be on their best behaviour and respond accordingly.

My first doggy holiday was with Sooty and Sweep. We booked a cottage near the top of the Sutton Bank just beyond Thirsk in the North Yorkshire Moors. We went in the first week in October because a) it was cheaper (my Lincolnshire breeding coming to the fore again), b) the dogs would be allowed on beaches after the summer curfew was lifted for the season, and c) the kids were all back at school and the countryside and woods would be quieter.

Chapter Seven

Thou shalt not leave the dogs on their own in the cottage, The Eleventh Commandment. So a whole weeks food, both dog and human had to go with us, because being on my own I was not going to be able to go out to the shops. Also included were all their beds, bowls and other bits and bobs, all squeezed into every nook and cranny within the car itself, because I had no boot to put it all in, that was occupied by two dogs. My luggage consisted of a holdall with a week's change of smalls and a couple of pairs of jeans etc inside, the rest of the stuff was all theirs.

We edged our way up the A1 out of Lincolnshire through Nottinghamshire and finally into Yorkshire. Stopping as near to every hour that lay-bys large enough and far enough from the carriageway allowed for letting two dogs out of the car. Sooty and Sweep would stay until told to get out of the boot and were pretty good around traffic, but there is always that chance with any dog, no matter how well trained, that they will take it into their heads to try playing with the vehicles for some reason or another, so they were put on a lead before they were allowed to get out.

We eventually found where we wanted to be after doubling back down the A1 thinking I had missed our turning and then deciding I was right in the first place, so the next exit was taken to turn round again. The cottage was fairly easy to find, but even then I had gone too far out of the village and had to be put right by someone cutting their front lawn.

The little cottage I had chosen from the brochure was a small converted barn, consisting of lounge, galley kitchen, one bedroom and a small shower room, snug and also very comfortable. That is apart from the approach, which was at the end of a half mile long stony and rutted track, certainly not designed for a Volkswagen Polo with a small engine to traverse along several times a day. It was very steep at one point, a first gear job, because I could not get any speed up to take a run at it due to the rutted surface. On the sweeping bend I had to be careful of the line I took or the exhaust would catch on the road if I did not avoid a steep dip on the right hand side, and a sharp grinding sound reminded me on the occasions when I was day dreaming.

The kitchen was only a very narrow galley affair, if there had been two of us, there was not even room to have an argument, so Sooty and Sweep had to eat their food outside the sliding door because there was just not the space for them in the kitchen itself with me as well. They didn't seem to mind as long as they were fed. They would wait just outside the door peeping round the jamb as I prepared their food and would back up as I came out carrying their bowls and take up their respective positions on their feeding mat, which had also gone with us. All the comforts of home, although I think they would have eaten their food off anything as long as it was in some form of bowl.

They were both more than a little unsure of themselves in their unfamiliar surroundings and a tad nervous of the whole situation, like ducks out of water, they followed me everywhere I went around the cottage. When we first arrived they religiously followed me in and out as I unloaded the car and dumped everything in the front room for now until I had time to sort it all out and find a place for everything, though I had to be especially careful where I put any eatables making sure they were placed well out of the reach of two inquisitive dogs. I sorted everything out when I had put the car in the nearby barn as requested by our host's instructions. Sooty and Sweep insisted on sitting on the settee with me when I was watching the television at night and followed me every time to the bathroom or into the kitchen. At night they would lay in the one basket together, despite there being two available placed at the side of the bed, and that had to be the one that was nearest to me. If the rules were going to be followed they were not supposed to be in the bedroom at all, there was no way they would accept sleeping in the lounge on their own, because they slept in the bedroom at home anyway and all my dogs have always done this.

Our first full day was the Sunday, and I took them to Scarborough. I had promised them when I had booked the holiday that I would show them Scarborough beach. Scarborough is my favourite seaside town on the Yorkshire coast. There is something charmingly magical about the old town and the harbour, with the castle looking down on you from all angles. I love walking round the harbour, particularly first thing in the morning before too many people are about, which I had the opportunity to do every morning before breakfast for a whole fortnight, as I took a holiday up there with the view to taking photographs because I was well into photography at the time, this was way before Sooty and Sweep were even thought of.

One evening during that fortnight, I had gone into town before dinner was due to be served at six, to get an evening local paper and look around the town. I had not taken the camera because I had already been out during the day taking photographs. As I walked through the main street there was a group of people gathered around a man who was playing "Scarborough Fair" on an accordion. I had seen him in several towns like Bridlington and Hull on previous visits to Yorkshire. He was blind and used a white stick for guidance. Passers-by would leave donations in his case at his side and then pause a while to listen to the harmonious melody. He was sat there on one of those brick built planters with seating, the evening sunlight streaming directly from behind him with the haunting notes floating away into the still and silent evening air. An excellent photo opportunity missed and gone forever, here is a case in point - "always carry a camera."!

One thing about Scarborough and any of the surrounding towns is everywhere you go there are steps. Thousands of them. Down to the beach and back up again. In Whitby there are one hundred and ninety nine of them up to the Abbey. The number of people who try counting them and get it wrong. If you want to get fit then take a week in Scarborough, you can't go anywhere without having to go up and down a flight of fifty odd steps. And if there aren't any steps then there are hills, and coming from the fens it is very noticeable.

Another quirk with this town is some of Scarborough's pubs on the harbour front are open first thing in the morning for the fishermen as they return to shore in the early hours to land their catch. I don't know what time the fishing vessels put in to port, but no matter how early I managed to get up I could never seem to get there soon enough to see them arriving. The seagulls are like monsters in size and are well used to humans and will sit tight until the last possible moment before taking to the wing, if at all, as you approach them. Some of the gulls even defied Sooty and Sweep. A sheep did that to Sooty once, as it went to butt her, she bolted off out of its way and wouldn't go near it or any others she came across thereafter. She could never be accused of sheep worrying!

The parking here was expensive - £3. I think that is the most I have ever paid for parking, certainly just to take the dog for a walk. But I was determined to have a photo of them both on the sand with the Grand Hotel in the background. In case you haven't guessed yet, being from Lincolnshire I am a bit careful with my money and do not like unnecessary spending, and this includes parking fees where it can be possibly avoided. I don't mind paying if I have to, but I would rather not if I can find somewhere free and will spend ages driving round and round sometimes which cannot be cost effective because I probably spend more in petrol than I am saving. I think the council get enough money out of me with the council tax. Which is probably why when on holiday I always seem to get the problem of people drawing up in vehicles to ask directions, because walking dogs up some side street they assume I am local and ask for directions to places I have never even heard of.

The Monday afternoon I took them round to the White Horse (a chalk figure on the hillside in the shape of a horse, not the nearest pub) and that was our first experience of the panorama off the bank top. It is unbelievably breathtaking, possibly the next best thing to flying with your feet still firmly on to the ground. All the cars approaching the bank look like little Dinky models. The view out over the moors is out of this world. It was a beautiful sunny and clear afternoon and you could see for miles. Even Sooty and Sweep were mesmerised, if it is possible for a dog to appreciate a view. I bet it is a beautiful sight in the snow, but I would hate to try and drive up here in the fluffy white stuff.

Because of their unfamiliarity of the territory, I did not want them to wander off and not be able to find their own way back. I did not want a repeat of the Incredible Journey, not with these two as stars anyway. At home they had been up almost every possible street they were likely to come across should they ever get out, but not here, so I kept them on extending leads all the time they were out on a walk. On the odd occasion I would relent, but made sure I kept a very close eye on both of them, and they were never allowed off when we were walking on a cliff top along either the bank or a coastal path. There have been several tales of woe from the past where an unleashed dog has slipped off the top of a cliff.

Most mornings I would take them in the car for a walk along the top of the Sutton Bank. You didn't have to pay for parking first thing! (Looking after the pennies...) There is a gliding club on the top of the bank, and every morning the grass runway was glistening with untouched dew in the crisp cold air. Except on the Thursday when there was a thick blanket of fog that just would not lift and hung there all day. I had planned to go into Thirsk that morning, and tried at around eleven; but lost my nerve because I was not familiar with the road and did not fancy those sharp bends in the road down the cliff side, especially as I could not even see the road for more than a few feet at a time in front of me, the fog was that thick you could not literally see the hand in front of your face. So I gave up and came back again.

Lorries could get themselves into difficulty at the best of times trying to get up the bank side and sometimes the police had to come to their rescue and close the road off so that they could back down again and have another go. I passed a low loader that had come to a grinding halt half way up and could not get the vehicle to move forward, every time he tried he just slipped ever further backwards. Getting passed him was tricky as it was a long vehicle and not too far from one of those hair pin bends. Cars towing caravans are just banned, they have to find another way round.

Thirsk is James Herriott country, as any fan will know, and had he still been practicing I would have made out one of them was ill just to be able to say she had been seen by a famous vet. I have always been a fan of his books. Skeldale House is now a museum to him and his books, with a fascinating array of exhibits from veterinary science's past. Well worth a visit.

Because it was so foggy that day I had taken them into a wood near the cottage for their morning walk, there was no point in driving to the bank top just to look at a grey shroud. As we ventured further into the wood we came to a clearing with hundreds of pheasants in it. Or so it seemed, there were birds all over the place, obviously a managed breeding area for shooting stock, a gundog's idea of heaven. Sooty and Sweep would have had a field day had they not been on extending leads, not that they were going to let such a minor detail stop them from trying, as pheasants scattered every which way. Sooty and Sweep could not decide which one they should chase first, never having seen so many birds in one wooded glade before.

Dalby Forest near Scarborough was also on the agenda for a visit, as so far I had only passed by on a bus and unable to stop and explore. Some might say when you've seen one woodland you've seen the lot. This is certainly not the case when you are a dog who likes to explore any new territory. One part of woodland can look pretty much like another and losing all sense of direction is not uncommon. I was a bit disorientated once on the way back to the car park and was going to go round a different way, but Sooty insisted we took this side path through the trees and would not be talked out of it. So I followed her and it brought us straight back to the car park. Just luck or did she know where she was, where she was going and how to get there?

We walked miles during the week on the Cleveland Way, in all directions north and south of Scarborough, to Whitby, Robin Hoods Bay and as far up as Runswick Bay. Robin Hoods Bay is a lovely little sea side village, a refuge to smugglers of the past, and you can see why. Nestled very neatly in the cliff side, ideal for cover at night for any dubious activity. It is a very steep climb from the sea front to the top of the cliff, and hand rails are provided, but you still need to be fit, because the only place to leave the car is at the top, and I would not like to try driving up there anyway. Not in my small engine car. If you want a walk on the shore and the little sand there is, the tide needs to be out, and you need to take care because it comes in fast and you can easily become trapped and unable to get back to the slipway, the only way off the sea front. The high sea walls are shear and unforgiving for any error of judgement.

They also had a look at all three levels of the Aysgarth Falls on the river Ure, that too tested the car engine climbing out of there in one go, especially for someone who does most of his driving in the fens. Both times I tried it I had to stop and put the hand break on tight half way up to stop the engine stalling. Bad driving? You try getting a small engine car up there in one go. There is probably a knack to it but I ain't blessed with it.

An article in a dog magazine had featured a walk starting in Goathland, Heartbeat Country. Just after we had started we met another dog who the owner had not put on a lead and it had a go at Sweep as they passed by each other. She retaliated but there was no bloodshed. "He usually gets on with other dogs." The number of times I have heard that one.

The rest of the walk went without incident. I passed another woman with a dog, on a lead this time, she said she had heard the scuffle and had put her dog on a lead for safety. Three hours later I was still popping dogs over stiles, carrying them over cattle grids, getting them unstuck from muddy patches, and getting myself stuck in the mud while unsticking them, only to find we had gone the wrong way and then had to get them and me back again through all that mud, unsticking them and then me all over again, but we finally made it back to the car.

The cocker will take everything in its stride, and they probably thought I was nuts, or probably even more convinced now than they were at the start of the day, but they followed me as faithfully as could be expected from any good dog in the face of adversity imposed on them by their owner. At a cattle grid I had to get both of them across by carrying them. The days when I could carry the pair of them together so that they were comfortable were long past. So I first took Sweep across, and instead of staying as told – Sooty did her level best to come with us. Fortunately she did not break any limbs before I had put Sweep down and gone back to her. But she had managed to make a valiant start bless her. Sweep looked at the possibility of following me, but I had Sooty over before she had decided how to try. She was not quite as adventurous as her sister.

According to the guide the whole walk was only supposed to take about an hour and a half. I had only paid for two hours parking, but either there weren't any traffic wardens or else it was his day off because we got away with it.

The week went far too quickly and we left the Sutton Bank at about 9am after having breakfast and taking the dogs for a walk along the bank top for a last look at that breathtaking view one final time. On what was a gorgeous sunny, lightly misted morning, which hovered just above the plain below us. As we walked, the ever warming sun evaporated forever this mysterious shroud, slowly giving up the hidden detail of the extensive plain. I didn't want to leave and wanted the walk to go on and on. So turning to walk back always marks a poignantly reluctant moment in a situation such as this, to which there is no return. And it is at times like these that I feel like just walking on forever, never turning round.

I drove them back, and after a quick cup of tea I loaded the car and handed the keys back to the owner. There was no point in hanging around, it would only make leaving all the harder. It had been a great week, we had walked miles, and the car had a total of over an extra thousand miles on the clock. We drove down that bumpy rutted track for the last time.

The only two that were overjoyed to be back when we finally pulled onto the drive were Sooty and Sweep. I think they had enjoyed their week but were glad to be back on their familiar territory and checked both house and garden to make sure everything was as it should be. They settled for a sleep when the car had been unpacked, the washing put on as there was loads of that, mostly mine, although their stuff did need a wash it was not as urgent as mine. After a quick lunch it was back to the usual routine, a walk and then back home for another sleep until it would be time for their tea.

They did return in the April of the following year. This time we stayed in the main house because my parents went with me along with their dog, a Sheltie called Blue. He usually got on well with Sooty and Sweep. But in case there were any disputes we took the cage to put the culprit in. It stayed folded up all week, because the biggest ruck was when Sweep took a swipe at Blue when he was pestering her to play and all she wanted to do was sleep because she had been on a long walk that day and was tired. With staying in the main house this looked out over the neighbouring farm and every morning I was woken to the bleating of sheep in the field just under my bedroom window. A world away from waking to the sound of passing cars. Since the arrival of Toby and Tasha holidays have had to cease because there are a very limited number of establishments that will take such a large number of dogs.

Chapter Eight

It was that year that the first attempt to breed from Sweep was made. I had already chosen the father to be, and arrangements with his owner had been made. Now it was a case of waiting for Sweep to oblige by coming into season which she would do in the fullness of her own time, and no amount of willing her, wishing and hoping or witch-craft was going to make a scrap of difference.

She was never that regular with her seasons and kept us waiting for over a month past her so called expected date. I had decided to have her blood tested on the recommendation of the father's owner, Keith. This is intended to indicate when the best day for mating is. So at day eleven she was booked into the vet to have a sample of blood taken. The results were negative, she was not ready. Which was not the result I wanted, but I was just impatient, and could not do a lot about it anyway except wait. So in two more days time she was back for another sample. The same. A further two days and she was "getting there" so her vet recommended that she was taken for mating on the Saturday.

So Saturday came and we made our way to Haxey to meet her intended. Sooty went as well, for the ride. Probably not the best of ideas, but she was a good girl and did not interfere; anyway she would have only been on her own if I had left her behind, and she went off with Keith's wife June out of the way quite happily. When they were put to each other Lenny was a lot taller than Sweep and unable to reach her properly. Cockers come in different sizes, and after this I will never look at a phone book in quite the same light again, because if the dog is taller than the bitch, one way to make up the difference so that she is the correct height for him is to stand her back legs on a phone book to "jack her up" a bit.

Despite several attempts to get them to mate, neither were that interested in each other despite the help of the BT publication. We then tried with a different dog, and even put them in a room together with a video camera set up so that we could see if they got down to it, and to give them some privacy in case they were feeling bashful. You might laugh but this can sometimes be the case. My Grandfather had taken one of his dogs to be mated and after several attempts with no success, he was going to bring his dog home. The other chap went to get something he was going to give my Granddad and while he was gone there was a tug on the lead and when he turned to look the two dogs were locked together, obviously thinking they had better get on with it or else their chance would be gone.

Sweep and Jasper however just walked around the room, looking in all the corners, and eventually both went to sleep, ironically in opposite corners. Tonight was certainly not the night. Keith suggested I left Sweep with them. That came as a total shock. Leave Sweep! Whilst I knew she would be well looked after, I was not prepared for this and the idea came totally out of the blue. No one had said anything about the possibility of having to leave her! I had expected to turn up, get Sweep mated, done and dusted, and bring her home. With any luck nicely in time for tea.

June, his wife, suggested I could stay the night as well if I wanted. I think she could see that I was not very keen on the idea of having to leave my dog. I declined because I would have to bring Sooty home as we had no dog food with us, and anyway I couldn't impose on them like that. Luckily Keith had some of the same food as Sweep had at home, so she would be alright for the night. Although this was not part of the plan, I left her in her cage with a blanket so that she would have a familiar smell of home to hopefully comfort her. I then drove Sooty home. She was like a duck out of water without her sister. Apart from a few hours whilst one or the other had stayed at the vet for one reason or another they had never been apart. Certainly not overnight, and when I stopped at a petrol station on the way home Sooty was looking all forlorn and very lonely in the back of the car.

I did not sleep a wink that night. I spent the whole night worrying about Sweep. It seemed like an eternity until a reasonable hour on the Sunday morning when I phoned to see how she was. I needn't have worried because she had slept soundly with another of Keith's bitches with them in their room for the night, had eaten her breakfast, gone out for a penny with all his other dogs, had run down the garden and back with them all, just as if that was what usually happened first thing every morning and what she had always done as if she had lived there all her life. Whilst this came as some relief that she seemed to be happy enough, I was still upset, and most of all I missed her enormously. I phoned Kathleen later to see if she had any advice as experience cannot be matched with any amount of theory that books have to give, she said that Sweep would mate when she was good and ready. I was just going to have to be patient.

In the middle of all this it was November the 5th. I had warned Keith and June about Sweep's fear of fireworks and they assured me they would keep an eye on her, but because she was in different surroundings she had not batted an eye lid and the night passed by without incident, in more ways than one. When she moved house the same applied, she did not associate the new surroundings with the noise and her fear of fireworks.

She was with Keith for a further three days before she finally mated with one of his dog's called Jasper; Lenny would still not do the business. So I fetched her home on the Wednesday afternoon after he had called to say that she had been mated the night before, I took the afternoon off work and Sooty also went with me to fetch her sister, she had been staying with my parents and Blue while I was at work, otherwise she would have been all on her own and may not have settled very well. I think she appreciated the company and she did get on with Blue. Sooty and Sweep were pleased to see each other and glad to be back together. Sweep's attitude towards her sister took on an immediate change, she made it plain that she was not going to take any nonsense, and Sooty just accepted the new regime. This was the first sign that Sweep gave me that she was pregnant. If you know your dog they usually give some subtle sign if you watch carefully.

At day forty I had Sweep scanned. She went to the vet on an out of hours appointment so that she was not near any other dogs and ran less of a risk of picking any infection up. Keith had told me to do this so I was just following advice. She was confirmed as pregnant. Up to that point it had been a guessing game of yes she was, no she wasn't as first of all she did something to suggest she was and then in the next five minutes something else which would indicate she wasn't. We were now on our way to the happy event.

As the due date for the litter drew ever closer, I was signed off with depression. I was so worked up and nervous about this whole pregnancy thing. It was this that actually tipped me over the edge and into my depressive state, but she certainly did not bring me up to that point, other factors such as stress at work were responsible for that. However she carried her pups full term was a miracle in itself because the bitch can take them back and reabsorb them if conditions are not right up to the point that the skeleton starts to form. My mood and actions would not have helped her cause, and if she suspected that something was not quite right or picked up an infection from somewhere, that could mark the end of her pregnancy. So it is best to keep a pregnant bitch away from other dogs and take them for walks in places little used by others, keep her as calm and relaxed as possible to guard against any complications. You also need to avoid bumping into her. In short I was having to panda to her needs for the nine weeks.

She started to give birth at about twenty to eight. Peter, a mate, had agreed to come over in an attempt to try and keep me calm as much as for any other reason. (On later reflection another bad idea.) I took the phone handset with us as I guided her upstairs. I rang Peter who was doing a stint for the Samaritans and said he would come over when he finished in about an hour. I also phoned Keith for a check on one or two points. In the meantime Sweep had started to give birth. I nervously watched as she strained and strained until she eventually gave birth to the first pup, a red girl with a very strange looking umbilical cord which took some breaking off, nothing like what people had said it would be like and strangely had two cords to it. Having never seen an umbilical cord before in my life I was sure this was what it was. What else could it be? Alas, what it turned out to be I discovered later, was the pup's intestines that had ruptured out of its stomach. So that one did not last long due to my ignorance. The only saving grace was that it may have been beyond saving before I made matters worse and would only have died anyway.

When Peter arrived he let himself in, as I had told him I would leave the door unlocked in case I was too busy with Sweep to answer when he arrived. He knew Sooty and she would not be likely to bite him. She had positioned herself quietly outside the bedroom door while Sweep had given birth to a further two pups and had stopped for the time being when he arrived. Bitches will often empty one side of the uterus and then have a bit of a pause before they start on the other. Keith had phoned a few times to see how things were going because he knew this was my first time of supervising a litter's birth. Sweep later commenced with the rest of the litter and by midnight she had six little puppies.

The happiness of the event was very short lived. After they were born she would not feed them and was reluctant to have much else to do with them. Again with my inexperience I did not notice there was a problem to begin with. When I did suspect something was not quite right I took her to the vet who showed me how to milk her, because there was certainly no shortage of supply, it was just that they would not suckle, and she was still reluctant to have anything to do with them. The vet having showed me how to draw milk off her, also gave me some substitute milk to mix up and try to feed the pups by bottle. She told me that they would need to be fed every hour. Then she took a look at me and I think she could see I was not coping and changed that during the night to maybe every two hours.

Things went from bad to worse as time went on. At three o'clock one morning when it had rang for the umpteenth time, I could have smashed the alarm clock that I had set to get me into gear to go and feed the pups. I was like a zombie as I went into the back bedroom and tried to get the pups to suckle from a bottle. I don't know if there is an art to this but I did not have it. Night after night of this and I was not coping. The litter did not last beyond a few days. One by one they died and one by one they had to be buried. It was because of ignorance on both sides as this was my first time as well as it was Sweep's. With my depression I was not able to think straight or deal with any kind of stress. This was not a recipe for success. After the last puppy had died I took Sweep downstairs. Sooty came to meet us and Sweep just went for her sister, I pulled her off and sat on the stairs with her, holding her tightly to me, and cried. What was the point?, it was all over now.

Sooty tried next; and this time I was better prepared for the possibility of having to leave her and took some of her food with us; just in case. She had one pup by caesarean section which died a few hours later because she was only reluctantly getting involved with the new arrival. When puppies are born naturally the actual passing of the pup through the birth canal kicks the Mother's instincts into gear, and this just hadn't happened here.

Chapter Nine

It came to a third attempt at a litter of pups, using Sweep. There is no way I would put Sooty through that again, even if her vet did agree after the caesarean. I desperately wanted one of them to have pups for one to keep. She went to a different breeder this time, and Sweep was using up the offer of a free mating from her sister's disaster, this is sometimes done when a mating is not successful, although some stud dog owners do not include the later failure of the litter. I took her on her own this time leaving Sooty with my parents and Blue. When we got there I could not find the bungalow to begin with as Keith had taken Sooty the first time round, so I had to phone the lady up for directions, (sat nav was not available at that time), she said she would send her partner to the top of the drive as she had seen us go past. It was a private road leading to an exclusive group of cottages built on the edge of a wood, so any strange cars driving along there were immediately noticed. There were probably at least a dozen pairs of eyes upon us as I drove slowly up and down trying to work out where I wanted to be.

After I had taken Sweep back up the lane for a penny, they soon got down to business and Sweep came home with me this time, and also nicely in time for tea as well. We returned forty eight hours later for a second covering with the same dog. This is sometimes done to try help ensure success, and I didn't want to leave anything to chance, because if it failed this time, Sweep at five was getting too old, and this was to be her last chance at Motherhood. The Kennel club rules are a bitch can be mated up to seven years of age. But even the second covering does not give any guarantees of success, although dogs are usually very fertile. I had bought a fertility crystal for her which she now had in a small pouch attached to her collar. Although it did not seem to be the getting pregnant bit I was having the problems with, it was the keeping them afterwards.

Sweep could be read like an open book this time, and within a couple of days I had a good idea that either she was pregnant again, or else she had convinced herself that she was. False pregnancies do happen and the bitch can go through all the motions which may include going into labour, before ultrasound scanning came in it was not impossible to have a case on the vets table for a caesarean before it was discovered that the bitch in question was not pregnant at all. They will also take their favourite toys around like pups and try to feed them. It is weird to watch a bitch that is affected by this and can be quite distressing for the owners, there is no real cure, you just have to sit it out and wait for her to stop. If the bitch is prone to doing this, one solution is to spay her before her next season. Anyway it was not with any surprise that the scan at day forty confirmed my suspicions because Sweep was giving all the right signs. Although I will add that they were nothing like the ones she gave the first time round. She also asked to go out to the loo at a different time in the night, I think this time it was eleven, just after I had gone to bed and settled to go to sleep, a black nose would appear over the edge of the bed and she would stand there whining until I got up again to let her out. Making sure she had been out for a penny before going to bed did not make a jot of difference. During her first pregnancy it had been three in the morning, as regular as clockwork, so I suppose I could be grateful it was a more respectable hour, but it would have been even better if she could have asked before I got into bed, but there you go, you can't have everything your own way, not at this game.

That was the year there was a foot and mouth outbreak, which in an uncanny kind of way was convenient because all the public footpaths were closed anyway, so it was down to street exercise only, and Sweep once she naturally slowed up did not want to be taken too far anyway. What I had to do with Sooty was take her out on her own for a longer walk. So they both went for a short morning walk, then when it came to the afternoon walk they both went out together as far as Sweep wanted to go and then I brought her back and got her settled on the settee, then I took Sooty out again for a walk of her usual distance. She was not keen on going out on her own, and kept very close to me, but she was not going to be deterred from the chance of a walk, and went, although be it slightly reluctantly and a little nervously without her companion. The Coronation Channel which skirted around the back of the town was still open to walkers so she and the rest of the town's dog population went round there. It is a total of five miles to do a complete circuit up one side and back down the other, which satisfied Sooty and did me good as well.

Before she was mated Sweep had been for an eye check (no – not with an optician and asked to read letters on a card) but with a participating vet in the PRA scheme (Progressive Retinal Atrophy). Cockers can be prone to this and it can be passed on to the pups if the Mother has the condition, so it is best to check if your bitch is afflicted. If they are unfortunately so, it will start to affect the night vision of the dog first, and then the vision at all light levels in advanced cases, so a quick test to guarantee the dog is clear before breeding is a good idea. Before the test is done the bitch has some drops put into her eyes and then in a dark room using an ophthalmoscope the vet looks into her eyes for signs of the condition. One of the vets doing the test, when he put the light out he could not find Sweep, I knew where she was because I had hold of her, he had to put the light back on and put a hand on Sweep before he turned the light out again.

On the way home from the testing venue we had to cross the A1, a very busy dual carriage way. When we drew up to the roundabout there were two lorries already in line waiting to go straight on as we were wanting to do. After several minutes and we had not moved an inch because the two lines of traffic coming from the south was just a constant stream, and likewise from the other direction so it was a case of waiting for someone travelling from the north to be going right to stop the flow and give you a chance to make a move. Anyway, as we continued to sit there I began to take an interest in what the paperwork that I had been given said, and started to read it. I became so engrossed in the content that it was not until sometime later I looked up and lo and behold the two lorries that had been sat there had now vanished and there was this massive gap yawning in front of us all the way to the dual carriageway. I took a quick look in the rear view mirror and there were two other vehicles behind me just sat there. Neither of them had bothered to just give a toot on the horn to wake me up. As you do when caught out like this I quickly drove up to the carriageway, feeling very sheepish.

Sweep was due to give birth on the Wednesday. Wednesday came and Wednesday went. Nothing. We got to Saturday, and true to form just after the vets had closed for the weekend, all hell let lose. She started to discharge this greenish fluid at about three in the afternoon, Sooty had done this and then dropped a dead pup, so I knew it spelt trouble. I phoned the vet on the emergency number and she said she would take a look at her. I drove her there and had to wait in the car park as we had arrived first.

When the vet arrived at the surgery she examined her, had a feel of her tummy area and decided to give her an ultrasound scan. She also called out a nurse because she was already planning on having to do a caesarean on Sweep. I was not keen on that idea after that had back-fired with Sooty, and made this none, but if it had to be done then so be it. She got me to complete a consent form to the operation before she told me to go home and she would phone me.

I went home, and when I got in I sat down and lifted Sooty onto my knee, she came to me as if she knew something was wrong and I was upset, I pulled her to me, hugged her, and I cried. Not a third time. No, not again. What was I doing wrong here? It was then that I turned my head to the heavens and told Him to stop messing about a let her have them. All I wanted was for Sweep to have pups, healthy little puppies with cute little faces, nothing elaborate, as all I wanted was a girl to keep, a girl from my Sweep, was this too much to ask? I must have done something really wicked in a previous life. Other people's dogs had puppies without a hitch, so why me?

I am not religious by any stretch of the imagination, but ten minutes later the phone rang. It was the vet. She had shifted a dead pup and ultrasound scanned Sweep. She had two more pups inside her that were still alive. So she had given her an injection to induce the birth and was sending her home for a while to give her a chance to give birth naturally, thinking she would be able to relax better at home in familiar surroundings. By this time my Mum had come round because I was so upset, I had phoned her because I had to talk to someone. She came with me to the vets and looked after Sweep on the way home.

I took Sweep upstairs, put her in the whelping box, and then sat on the bed and waited. I didn't have to wait long. She moved out of the whelping box and into the big basket before giving birth to a gold boy. And then things seemed to come to a halt. I did take the pup out of the basket and placed it in a cardboard box on a fleece blanket with a hot water bottle underneath to keep things snug and warm in there, when she looked like she was going to give birth to the other one. She promptly stormed out of the bed, roughly grabbed hold of the pup in her mouth and took it back into the basket, she handled it so roughly that it squealed out loud as she moved it, but that didn't deter her, she put it back in the basket behind her where it was in the first place before I started to interfere, and turned to look at me as if to say "Now if you want to try that again I am ready for you". That was me told!

I remember my Nan doing her nut once when Judy had a litter of pups. That is if people of that age could do such a thing. Judy would not let my Grandfather near her and she was his dog. She was very protective of her family. I was playing outside in the yard and it began to spit with rain, so instead of going into the house I for some reason decided to get into the kennel. It was built so that there was a front compartment where Judy's water bowl was and where she was fed of an evening. Then there was a partition and over that was her bed of straw. I went into the front compartment and sat there leaning over the partition stroking Judy while looking at the pups. She was not bothered in the least by my presence. When my Nan found me in there she went mental. I wondered what all the fuss was about and I think Judy was a bit bewildered.

After another hour with nothing happening I phoned the vet again. By now it was eight o'clock at night. She agreed to have another look at her, and gave her another birth inducing injection, and sent her home again.

It was a five minute drive back home, especially at that time of night. When I had pulled onto the drive I opened the boot, Sweep got out and went inside, like nothing had happened. We then lived in a small cul-de-sac which was a little sparse on street lighting, the single street light was some way away from my drive. So it was by sheer luck that I spotted this black thing in the car boot and picked it up wondering what it was. It was very hot, to the point that it nearly made me drop it again. Christ! It was a pup!

I raced indoors after Sweep, she seemed totally unconcerned about the pup she must have just a few seconds ago given birth to and left in the car boot. But she took to it when I placed it with her along with the boy. The new pup promptly inched her way to the milk bar – elbowed the obstruction out of the way – this was her brother who had just settled himself onto the best teat. She just knocked him off it and attached herself to the teat. He had to find himself an alternative feeding station. So she was not going to take any nonsense off nobody.

The black girl was Niki or Nikita, Jack's grandMother.

The next day I was back at the vets. Fleas. The pups had fleas. Flea eggs can live in a carpet for up to three years waiting for the right time to hatch, and two new unprotected pups were ideal. The vet gave me some Frontline spray which you can use on puppies from one day old. That cured the problem within half an hour. To be on the safe side I treated both Mother and Aunty, although Sooty was not allowed near them. Sweep had to be kept away from the pups until the flea treatment had dried into her coat and theirs, because neither of them were allowed to lick each other whilst the treatment was still wet. Sooty did make one attempt to try and see what her sister had got, but Sweep was having none of it and growled a warning across Sooty's bows, which she heeded and went back downstairs where she was spending all her time at the moment. But in true Cocker style she just accepted the situation and slept alone down stairs for the next three weeks without question or protest. I tried to give her as much love as time would allow because I did not want her to feel left out, but she seemed to be coping admirably, she was getting her walks and fed. Maybe she was quietly relieved the pups were her sister's, and therefore Sweep's responsibility to look after them, almost like a grandMother, pups are OK when they are someone else's and can be given back.

She did not even bother to get involved with the pups when they came down stairs after their eyes had opened and they were weaned. As I had again been signed off with depression there was no problem of what to do with her whilst I was out at work. Sooty did make sure that they all knew she was still boss mind. Particularly with the girl, Niki, because she saw her as the threat. She did not bother so much with Prince, he was a boy and no challenge to her as the head bitch.

I eventually breathed a sigh of relief after the two of them had had their second injection. Now they were fully protected and ready to go out and face anything the big wide world was going to throw at them. I took them round to my Mum and Dad's most days so that they would get used to meeting another dog, their dog Blue. He was very good with them because he was very boisterous with Sweep and always played with her when she visited, but he just sat at a distance and looked at the pups. I think he thought they were too small and fragile to play rough and tumble with. He only made a move to play when they first approached him. After that there was no stopping him.

Puppies seemed to fascinate him because when Jack and Arran

first came down stairs they spent a lot of time in the puppy pen, and when he was visiting he would sneak quietly into the kitchen and just sit and watch them as they stared back at this strange looking dog that was sitting there staring at them, neither side willing to give in first.

Up until Niki's arrival, Sweep had always been Blue's favourite, and they played together every time they met. Sooty could not be bothered with such childish games and did not get involved. When Niki arrived and started to play with Blue, Sweep was given the elbow, a woman scorned by her own daughter. And despite her trying to say hello to Blue he would just turn his head and ignore her. He now only had eyes for Niki. So fickle.

Prince was the first dog to show an interest in the drinking of tea. He came over and sniffed at the cup so I found a saucer and put some down for him. He drank it down quickly, hoping for a second helping. His sister curious to see what he was getting that she wasn't, came over to investigate, so I gave her some on a saucer, she drank it readily too. Sooty and Sweep had never asked for any and showed no interest now, but some dogs will drink tea. Prince after he had left home helped himself to Danny's beer. Danny had put his glass of beer down beside his chair and when he went back to it, most of it had gone with Prince looking woozy in the corner probably wandering why the world was suddenly going round in circles. That was his last taste of that because Danny, like me, did not believe in letting dogs drink beer. And if Prince had a sore head in the morning then that was his own fault. Toby likes tea and will hold the cup between his paws and tilt it towards him to make sure he gets every last possible drop. Our first ever dog, Lucky, would only drink it if it had two sugars in it, and she soon cottoned on who had the required amount in their tea, she never asked my Mother who did not have sugar, she would drink it at a push if it was all that was available but she was not keen. If they are given it and it is a bit hot, they have the good sense to wait a few minutes before trying again to see if it has cooled down by now.

Niki's brother, Prince, left home at just after his twelfth week. Several people had shown an interest in him but none of them seemed to be suitable to me. I would stand there talking to them and all the while thinking "well there is no way you're having him" maybe I was being too fussy about who ended up with my dog, but damn it, it had taken enough effort to get him on the planet. Then a friend who knew about the litter put me in touch with Danny who only lived just around the corner from us, so he had seen me taking them out for a walk on puppy leads. The same leads I had bought for Sooty and Sweep. At first I had reservations that if he was going to be living just round the corner then I could potentially see Prince at any time, and would this be too emotional for me? But Danny and his wife seemed as perfect as possible owners that if this was the only problem, then it was a selfish one on my part, and the interests of Prince had to come first. He went to his new home with Danny on the Saturday morning, in the usual laid back manner of the Cocker Spaniel, he just sat in the front seat of Danny's car and went off quite happily to his new abode. When they had both come round to look at him the night before, they had asked if he could just go home with them for a short time to see how he settled. I walked back the short distance with them with Prince on his lead. It did not seem to bother him that he was on his own and his sister was not with him. He went straight in and onto the nearest settee. No problem about making himself at home then. We had a cup of tea and he just lay down and went to sleep. Perfectly happy. Danny wanted to leave any final decision until the morning; he wanted to have a word with his wife, Alex, to make sure they were both thinking the same, so he came home again for the night.

His last night at home as it turned out, as Danny phoned in the morning to say that they would take him if I was still willing to sell. We agreed that he would write me a cheque, he wanted to get me cash, but I was not walking to the bank with a wodge of notes like that in my hand. Anyway I would not have far to go if the cheque bounced! Danny also wanted a bit older pup that had already had all its inoculations so that he could take him to work with him. He worked for the RAF and the MOD would only accept the dog onto their premises if he had been fully inoculated and had the necessary paperwork to prove it. As we sorted out all the paperwork on the top of the fish tank, I handed Danny the inoculation certificate which as I remarked, "That should keep the MOD happy."

When he went it was easier than I had thought it would be to watch him go. He departed quite happily with a few days' supply of food to give Danny time to get organised and buy him some, this is usual practice to new owners. Talking of feeding, when they are twelve months old they are supposed to move off puppy food, and if you have bought a puppy and want to change to a different brand of food this is a good time to do it, that is what I did with Sooty and Sweep as they were on tinned puppy food when they arrived, and I had decided to feed them on complete. Any changes that are made have to be done gradually, even with the same brand, then you minimise the risk of upsetting their tummies. With Sweep in particular, I only had to think about changing her food to upset her.

Chum do a junior food which is for dogs aged from twelve to eighteen months. When I moved Sooty and Sweep on to this they were fine with it and liked it. However when it came to Niki changing from puppy, I went out and bought her a twenty kilo bag of junior food, I also got Danny a bag because he wanted to feed Prince on complete food as well. When I tried to introduce Niki to it she didn't want to know, and ironically neither did Prince. So that was two whole bags of food that went to waste. Well the RSPCA did alright out of it, and Niki was put straight onto adult. The only saving grace was that I did not have to buy two types of food from now on, which made both shopping and feeding a whole lot easier and cheaper.

Chapter Ten

A nd so now there were three. Niki went out in the car for the first time with Sooty and Sweep on the afternoon of her brother's departure. She was overjoyed to be going out with the adults at last, and showed no remorse whatsoever at the departure of her brother. I kept her on an extending lead because she had not been taught the recall yet. All she wanted to do was run after the others, but she kept coming to the end of the lead. So next day we took them all to the beach at Chapel St Leonards and with a hand full of dog treats it took ten minutes to teach her to come to me when called. The only problem was that Sooty and Sweep also cottoned on that there were treats in the offing and also started answering when "Niki" was called. Had there been any other dogs around at the time who noticed what was going on, I would no doubt have had them answering to "Niki" as well.

When I first started walking Sooty and Sweep I used to keep them on extending leads, too nervous to let them off in case they did not come back. It was not until I had had them for some time that someone said to me that I needed to let them off before they made up their minds that they did not need me anymore. So on the Coronation Channel where I could see well ahead that there were no other dogs about, I tried letting Sweep off first. Sooty could be a bit headstrong and would choose not to listen if suited her not to. Sweep was well behaved and came back when called. A few days later I tried with Sooty. She was also fine, in a fashion; well at least I didn't lose her. Now and again she would just take off at will and not respond to any amount of calling her back. Sweep never did this except for once when I really hadn't looked at the dog beside me and just assumed the one that had run off to be Sooty. After several calls and still no response I looked down at the dog beside me, which was Sooty looking very bewildered wandering why I was shouting her to come back when she was already here? One call of

"Sweep" and the dog in the distance instantly responded. It was no use trying to whistle because I am one of those people who cannot do so for toffee. The first time I did try to whistle Sooty and Sweep to get their attention, they both looked at each other wondering what that strange sound was and were looking bewilderedly around for wherever it cometh from.

I did invest in a proper dog whistle. I purchased said item from a gun shop. I phoned them up from work before going round there to see if they sold ultrasonic dog whistles? "No, but we do sell silent ones."!

Now Niki was on her own she spent her first night upstairs with her Mother and Sooty. She had already learnt how to get up and down stairs on her own from copying the adults, as pups do if there are any around to show them how it is done. Up until now her and her brother had both been sleeping downstairs in the puppy pen. The reason for doing this was because in case any potential new owners decided they were not going to allow the dog to sleep upstairs because not everyone does.

My reasoning for sleeping them with me is because just before I took ownership of Sooty and Sweep a house just round the corner caught fire during the night. The chap had been out for a drink and when he came home he went to bed and left the dog downstairs. He did manage to get out, just. The dog was not so lucky and died in the fire. My line of thinking is that if the animal is with you, it will be able to wake you by jumping onto the bed if necessary and giving you valuable time to get out. Far better than any smoke alarm as the battery is not going to fail. When you keep two or more, there is always one of them that is only cat napping and alert, as they would do in the wild they take it in turns to keep watch, and will thus wake the others should the need arise to warn of any approaching danger. I found though that with Sooty and Sweep, particularly Sweep, that as she got older she was no longer included in this rota.

I saw Niki's brother and his new owners the next day. They said he had been alright during the night and seemed to have settled into his new surroundings very well. Although with all the houses being of the same design there would not be a lot of difference in respect of him knowing where everything was, and no matter where they are taken, all dogs can seem to manage to find the kitchen without too much difficulty. Cockers are usually pretty happy providing they are fed watered and taken for a walk. It seemed like the two siblings were not that bothered about being separated, which was not a bad thing. I think Sweep was pleased to see the back of him, because she looked at Niki when he had gone as much as to say "Right that's him gone – now, when are you going?"

Shortly after taking Prince cum Bungle (Danny's wife's choice of name, or she got the blame), Danny bought another Cocker bitch, Truffles, a chocolate coloured pup, who had been kennel bred. She was very nervous of things like the television and the hoover. This is the problem with kennel bred pups that have not been introduced to the general hubbub of the house, they are not used to household appliances and it takes them time to adapt. She would follow Bungle's lead though, which would help her. When Sooty was covered for the second time the dog came to her at Keith's, and the television had to go off because the boy lived outside and had never seen one, and it was putting him off. Keith was not best pleased as he was trying to watch the football. He was later banished from the room because he kept shouting at his dogs for doing some mis-demeanour or other and again it was putting the dog off. He was only allowed back in when they were tied together.

With a litter that have been reared in the home they are already used to the noises generated by the usual household appliances and make better house dogs. Although for some reason Sooty and Sweep would always retreat into the kennel whilst I scooted the hoover round the lounge. This did have its advantages because there is nothing worse than a dog either always in the way, one that won't move, or one that is always chasing the brush. Many a time I have to go back to the spot Tasha was laid on and refused to be moved from.

Truffles, being a bitch, in the fullness of time, did what all bitches do and came into season. Bungle still having all his tackle started to show a definite interest. Danny wanted to get Bungle castrated, but the vet could not do it straight away as he wanted, and that would not have made any difference anyway, a castrated dog is still capable of getting a bitch pregnant for several weeks after the offending tackle has been removed.

To avoid an unnecessary mating he asked if I could have Truffles and he wanted Niki to go to him to keep Bungle company. There was no way I could be away from Niki's coat for three whole weeks, she needed daily attention as she was currently being shown, so he had to settle on Sooty. So Truffles came to us for three weeks, Sooty seemed to take the new arrangements in her stride, that was why I agreed to her going, and Truffles certainly did. Sweep would not have settled so well if she had gone to Danny's, despite Bungle being her son.

Niki saw her opportunity immediately; Truffles arrival meant she was no longer the underling. Suddenly she had a dog below her and took full advantage of making that fact more than obvious and bullied Truffles something rotten. It was not all plain sailing for Bungle either, he apparently tried to play with Sooty who did not do puppies at the best of times, so she made her feelings known right from the start by nipping him on the ear. Just like Queen Victoria, she was "not amused." Although she did not seem to mind the new arrangements I think she was pleased to be back home when Truffles finished her season and I think Bungle was pleased to see his play mate back again.

Having the dogs around was a definite advantage to me and my wellbeing whilst I was down with depression. If I had not had them there were days when I just would not have bothered to get out of bed in the mornings, and certainly days when I would have just ended it. But I had a responsibility to my dogs, they were not going to take no for an answer and still needed feeding and walking. I would on some days get up, feed and walk them, and then go back to bed for the rest of the morning. I was not alone for long and they would come up stairs and went to sleep in their baskets with me. They would look quizzically at me at times, but they would just accept the situation and go to sleep beside my bed. They dragged me out in the afternoon though, which could only be good for me to get out in the fresh air, and once started I did go for a decent distance which took at least an hour. The exercise and fresh air also helped to make me sleep better at night, which was one of my main problems. I was going to bed to go to sleep for about ten minutes before waking and tossing and turning for the rest of the night, tired but unable to sleep.

My depression lasted for three months before I was well enough to return to work. When I did Niki would have to be outside in the kennel with Sooty and Sweep. As the boss, Sooty was still exerting her authority on the new arrival at every opportunity, as she saw her as a threat to her position, and therefore determined to make sure the pup knew her place. I would have to separate them when they were left in the kennel for the time being, so I borrowed an extending garden trellis from next door and put it along the centre of the pen and the kennel. It was not ideal but it did the job and kept them apart until Niki was big enough to look after herself if necessary or Sooty accepted her in the kennel, whichever came first. Niki just showed Sooty respect accepting that she was the underling, and there was no real physical conflict between them.

Niki was introduced to the show ring at a small open show in King's Lynn. She went on her own. I took a cage so that she would have her own space and no one would stand on her if there were a lot of people around. She went into the cage willingly, lay down and promptly went to sleep. She didn't even bother to protest when I walked off to look at all the stalls that were set up around the walls of the hall selling all things doggy. She did get anxious once at a show when she lost sight of me. I had left her with Sooty for company, with a cage each to go into if they wished. I had two cages set up because Sooty would not have accepted the pup in the same cage as her. Someone at the ring side tried to calm her down, but she was having none of it until I reappeared when Sweep had finished her class. That was the last time Sweep went to a show because half way round she sat down and would not move. She had not wanted to go in the first place, and decided to enforce her protest with a sit in, so there ended her show career.

Niki did very well in shows as a puppy. At Crowland Companion Show the puppy class was so large they had to split it into two, all the table dogs, that is all the small dogs, were seen first, then they had to go out of the ring whilst the non table dogs were judged. There were twenty-six puppies in all, although how some of the non table dogs could be called puppies was a mystery because if they were puppies I would hate to meet the adult version in a dark alley. It took the judge an hour and a half to go through them all. Niki was awarded first, and also got best puppy. I could not believe it; my little girl had been awarded first out of so many dogs. She did the same at Wansford in England, although there were not as many puppies there, they still had a fair number of entries. Bags of food where also given to the winner as part of the prize, and for the six months she was eligible for puppy classes, I hardly had to buy her any food.

The farthest she travelled to a show was the other side of the Humber, I had entered her because the person judging had placed her Mother well in previous shows, so I wanted to see what he thought to the pup. It was a waste of time because Niki was the only dog entered in her class, but like Sooty and Sweep she could claim she had been across the Humber Bridge.

Between Niki and the arrival of her pups, Tasha and Toby, we moved. I wanted a house with a large garden, which meant looking at older or ex local authority properties. The only thing with ex local authority is they tend to be terraced and the whole row has access across the back between your back yard and the garden. A no no if you own a dog. You need to be able to let the dog out and know it is safe, without having to accompany them all the time.

It came to moving day and the three of them went to my parents first thing so that they were out of the way. Moving can be stressful enough without having to keep a tight rein on three lively gundogs. They were not over happy with the arrangement, but in true Cocker style accepted the situation. They were pleased to see me at dinner time while I waited for the keys to the new house to be handed in to the estate agents. And protested loudly when I disappeared again without them. When they eventually arrived at their new residence and first saw the garden which is nearly two hundred feet in length, I don't think they could quite believe that it was all theirs, and explored it further and further down very cautiously to begin with. My Mother's dog Blue never did venture down the whole length of the garden, even if she went down there, he would only accompany my Mother so far, then he would stop and wait for her to come back.

One time I took the three of them to visit our old neighbours, Sooty got out of the car and ran with glee up her old path to the gate. She was disappointed that she was not going in or staying. I could never work out whether they were happy with the move or not, or whether they just accepted the situation for what it was. Fred and Molly were the best neighbours anyone could ask for. We were neighbours for eight years and moving away from them was one of the main reasons that made the move a sad affair. Molly suffered badly with arthritis and spent a lot of time unable to get downstairs despite having a stair lift fitted. She used to have injections once every three months and then was fine for a while, but the time that she was confined to bed became longer and longer. It was several years after moving that I saw someone else from the same cul-de-sac at Heckington Show, who told me Molly had died and Fred had moved back to London to be near his family. She said that the death of Molly affected him really deeply, and that he was unable to cope on his own. While she was alive Molly was the one who dealt with all the affairs of the running of the house. They would look after the dogs for me during the day and always bought them some treats for Christmas. She is sadly missed. And it is times like this that make you stop and think how strange some situations in life can be, like with Fred moving back to London, we will never meet again, ever.

Chapter Eleven

Before Niki was given the chance of pups we rented a cottage for a week situated near Caldbeck right on the northern edge of the Lake District National Park. The week did not get off to a very promising start weather wise. Making our way up north it rained all the way. At one point I had to pull over onto the hard shoulder of the A1 because it was raining so hard the wipers were not coping with it, even on their fast setting, making it impossible to see where I was going. I was not the only one that had stopped until the rain decided to ease a little; the hard shoulder was like a car park for several miles as the storm progressed ever slowly northwards. We finally found Faulds Farm and the farmhouse with the attached terrace of two little cottages just beyond the village itself, half way up a gently rising hill that carried on to a steeper series of stepped rises to where it levelled to the road junction at the summit.

When taking three dogs you cannot be too choosey about the choice of location, it is a case of selecting an area and then finding someone mad enough to accommodate that number of animals in their property and making the best of a bad job as it were. And that inevitable sentence in the cottage write up at which I always cringe "Well behaved dogs welcome" yes, right, as I look at the three of them, at least they answer one part of that, they are dogs.

After unpacking the car of everything, including the dogs, in the pouring rain which I am sure had tracked with us hovering above our heads all the way up here, I prepared our teas, arranged all their bedding and covered the furniture as part of the routine. It was still pouring down with rain outside when I closed the curtains for the night, and the stream that was running down the side of the road carrying the runoff water down the hill, was still bubbling past the front door. The cottage was warm and cosy, helped by a real coal fire. This was a long forgotten novelty for me as I had not experienced an open fire since childhood, and the dogs had never seen one at all, but that did not bother anyone, they soon cottoned on to its advantages, and there was a bit of a jostle for the front pew. So every night, cold or not, I lit the fire, and just the sight of the burning embers made me feel instantly warmer. Watching the dancing flames brought back the memories of that old game on cold winters nights of watching the flames and seeing pictures in the glowing embers. Some dogs will also sit and watch the flames, Lucky would do it a lot and Tasha will sit there looking into the embers, I wonder if they can also see images in there? Stuff your central heating, half the fun used to be in getting the fire lit ASAP to get warm, along with the bit where it went out at least once and the frantic scrabble to relight it because it was cold! And that dangerous act of holding a newspaper in front of the grate opening to get it to draw, my Nan was always having to put the paper out on the hearth. She would also light the fire in one room and when that was going take a shovel full of burning embers through to the grate in the other room. Health and safety eat your heart out!

When on holiday on my own with the dogs I would save a lot of money because shopping is out of the question as the dogs are always with me, and apart from a quick trip into the local shop for milk or other perishable essentials while they have to wait in the car, spending sprees are off the agenda. I miss all the main attractions because I am looking for places to take a number of dogs where there are as few people and other dogs as possible, which generally ends up being the out of the way places no one else hardly ever visits. I save on the car parking as well because the chances are that wherever is so remote there is no charge. A lot of beauty spots have "honesty boxes", and while I did leave the recommended amount I bet there are people who don't bother.

From the top of the hill above the cottage, I could look down on the farm spread out beneath us and the village beyond; I also had to go up there to get a signal for the mobile phone which was not available from down the hill near the cottage. All phone calls had to be made when the dogs went out for their morning walk when we got to the top of the hill. I could spend ten minutes on the phone while trying to keep an eye on three loose dogs and any traffic, not as though there was much of that to deal with. A school mini bus would wend its way between all the farms picking the children up, and I would watch it every morning on its route. Climbing up that hill every morning kept us fit, coming from the fens none of us, dogs and all, were used to these kinds of gradients. It was from up here that I could look back out across the valley to the snow capped High Peak behind us. The sun would first catch the tops of the mountains and the valleys would still be in shadow. The air had a definite nip to it when out of reach of the sun's rays first thing, and the day had to be well aired before the warming rays reached into the valley bottom at this time of the year. A pause at the hill top gave an opportunity to benefit from the warmth before returning back into the valley. The same effect could be found first thing in the morning on the Sutton Bank, we would be walking along the ridge in brilliant sunshine while the plain below us was still in shadow, and I could follow my own shadow and those of the dogs crossing the valley floor beneath us. Those of you that live in such places are probably wandering why I am making such a meal out of this phenomena, but to someone who comes from the fens where the sun gets up everywhere at once, this is quite a novelty to watch as the sun advances slowly over the land below.

It was spring, so there was an abundance of little lambs in all the fields close to the farm house and the older ones out on the fells all around. Everywhere I looked there were Sheep feeding one or two lambs, some even had three. A sight that confirms spring has arrived and winter is now behind us. There were times when the roads were blocked with sheep being moved from field to field, but they take priority up here and motorists just have to be patient. This is sheep country; there are sheep everywhere you turn. One shepherdess moving a small flock up a hill to a top field started off with her woollen hat on at the bottom of the hill, by the time she got to the top this had been removed, hot work moving sheep uphill, even for the professional hill walkers.

Our first outing of the week was to the top of Great Dodd. Eight hundred and fifty seven metres above sea level, starting in woodland it was a gradual climb for the dogs so they coped with the gradient okay as the path gently rose upwards, the trees continued to thin until we reached the summit poking out above the tree line like a bald top, it is the highest point we as a group, me and them, or even individually, have ever stood on. Not like when we tried Pen-Y-Ghent and had to give up because they are dogs, not mountain goats. The view from the top of Great Dodd was disappointing when we made it to the top because it was foggy and you could not see very far below us at all. But never mind the aim was to get to the top. The descent was far easier. To begin with gravity was on our side. And on the way down we passed a family and the chap who was leading with his son said to me what nice looking dogs they were, and added that his wife may burst into tears when she saw them but did not say why, When she got to them she also commented on how nice they looked but didn't burst into tears, and to this day I do not know why she should have because he did not venture an explanation, and can only surmise why.

Some of our destinations in the rest of the week found us taking short journeys along the M6, and I was amazed when at times we were the only vehicle in sight. The last time I had seen a motorway as empty was the A1 when the petrol dispute was on. It was the weekend we were coming home from Kirby Malzeard and there were three cars to be seen on the whole motorway – one in the distance up front, one in the distance in the rear view mirror and mine. I could drive in any lane I chose. Several times when we used the M6 it was virtually devoid of other vehicles. We drove over the highest point on the motorway at 1050 feet (or 320 metres for the metric boffins) above sea level as it runs over Shap Fell, one of the highest points on any motorway in the UK. It is also here that the north and south bound sections of the motorway divide for a number of miles to help cope with the extreme weather conditions up here in the winter. One beautiful and clear sunny morning on the M6 we passed a prison van on a wide sweeping bend with the sun in my face as it was warming the previously chilling air. I couldn't help thinking how sad for any occupant(s) to be missing out on the enjoyment of this glorious day. Not really considering what they may/may not have done to be in there in the first place.

The coast and the Solway Firth were not far away from base, so we had several trips up there and walked along the beach just to look at the coast on the west side of the country instead of the east side all the time. From the beach near a small coastal town called Silloth you can look out over the Solway Firth and towards the shore across the vast expanse of water to Scotland's wooded coastline and rising hillside opposite. We had a trip to a quiet part of Morecambe and took a long walk out onto the vast sands of Morecambe Bay. A petrol station there nearly caused an accident, because their prices were really cheap, as I slammed on the brakes spotting the bargain at the last minute to make an emergency right turn for the entrance. At those prices we were having some of that!

We also had an afternoons walk in Galloway Forest. One woodland is pretty much like another, especially when you are not a dog, but they enjoyed themselves and it made a change from the usual woodland walks. I chose them a quiet spot before letting them all out of the car; they were on their extending leads mind, as a dog does not have to stray far in woodland before it has disappeared from view. There is no going to sleep while walking three of them on extending leads, if knots are to be avoided that is. A keen eye has to be kept on the dogs as they change places with each other and the same has to be done with their leads, made ever more difficult to follow because the lead cords are the same colour- black- and at times there are frantic attempts to unravel them first one way then the other. It is like juggling swapping lead handles from one hand to the other and back again to try and keep pace with them. Some bright spark has come up with a black and white coloured cord and that does make it easier to work out which lead is which.

There was logging work going on, and the road we ended up coming back out on was really muddy as there were lorries going in and out all the time churning at the road surface. The dogs' feet and everything else close to the ground (pretty much most of the dog) was really muddy by the time we found the car again. Waiting for it to dry and drop off them would have taken days, time I didn't have. I didn't want them going back to the cottage all muddied up like that. There was a stream near to where I had parked the car, so I put them all in it to get them cleaned up. I don't know what the environmental impact was downstream though, because the water bubbling on its merry way went very murky for a time.

Apart from the journey up there the weather gave us a decent week. It was cloudy some days but it hardly rained. On our last day they went for a walk along a section of Hadrian's Wall as it was fairly close and just to say we had been there. Sooty and Sweep were used to me taking their photos and both of them would stay sitting where I told them while I walked back a bit to get them in the shot. Sooty would look bored in several photographs, you can tell she was thinking "Will he get on with it." Niki never did take to the stay bit and consequently there are no photographs with her in them. I am sure there are a few kicking around somewhere with Sooty and Sweep in front of this ancient Roman monument.

Towards the end of the week I think Sweep was getting tired, coming back down a fairly steep wooded hillside it had started to drizzle with rain, now there is a novelty for the Lakes, so I hurried them along as I do not like them to get wet if it can be avoided, especially as we were in rented accommodation as a wet Cocker has a bit of an unpleasant aroma to it until they are dry and to get there they will wipe themselves against everything in sight. It was not until I had got back to the car that I noticed Sweep was not with us. After calling and calling her, I closed the boot down after putting the other two in there to keep them out of the rain; I retraced my steps and found her about half way back up the slope curled up. I picked her up and carried her back to the car. That was the last full day so she would be going home tomorrow.

On the flip side of the coin we had a really dreadful week in the Yorkshire Dales one time. Apart from two days it otherwise rained for the whole week. It did more than rain; the wind was relentless as well. In fact the only reason the rain was hitting the ground was because the ground was a forty-five degree slope, had it been flat the rain would have been going parallel to the ground because the wind was blowing that hard. Even Sooty did not object to not going out in it for a walk. I just had to open the door and show her outside to get her to change her mind. One time on one of the more "acceptable" days we had gone up to the Ribblehead Viaduct, I had stopped the car and opened the door to get out, when the wind snatched it from my grasp and slammed it in the open position with such force it is a wonder it did not fetch it off its hinges. I let the dogs out for a quick walk round and put them quickly back into the boot. Despite the sun being out it was impossible to walk against this force of nature that was not going to stop for anyone, man or beast.

Chapter Twelve

Tasha and Toby's arrival was pretty uneventful. Niki gave birth to them without incident at about six in the morning, not a bad time from a selfish point of view. I can cope with that time of the morning better than half way through the night. She just did what a Mother had to do and got on with the job in hand of giving birth. I had to start Toby breathing and nearly exploded his lungs because I blew far too hard into his muzzle having never done this before I was unsure how hard I had to blow, obviously not as hard as that. It made him splutter a bit, but he got over it. He has been nothing but trouble since and there are times when I wish I hadn't bothered.

That night I decided to sleep in the kitchen to be with her and the pups in case she wanted anything, or something went wrong. By four in the morning I had had enough, I could not get to sleep so decided to go and have a couple of hours in bed. When I came down next morning, my heart stopped. Niki had finely shredded all the newspaper in the whelping box and the pups were nowhere to be seen. I quickly bundled Sooty and Sweep outside, treading cautiously myself as I did not want to stand on a pup. I turned to search through the paper for the pups. I soon found them, alive, amazingly, and they seemed to be okay. I put them back in the whelping box and Niki went to inspect them and feed them, and they responded to her presence and had a good feed, seemingly unaware of the panic I had just had. Why she did what she did I do not know. During the day I moved the whelping box, pups and her into the back bedroom so that I could hear her or the pups during the night if needs be. After that she settled quite contentedly as if that is just what she wanted, because in the wild some animals will move their young to a new location shortly after giving birth so that the smell from the birthing fluids does not attract any unwanted predators.

The trouble with these two started as they got older. Tasha has always been my worst escapologist. A little Houdini that one. When she was still a puppy I wanted to put her and her brother outside in the kennel, so I set to and built a pen. I did not want one with wire so opted for wicket fencing. She had other ideas. I left her and Toby outside in the pen with water and the kennel open for them to go in if they wanted and also for shelter if it rained. When I came home at lunch time I was greeted at the garden gate by the two pups. They had got out, somehow. After checking the fencing and trying twice more to leave them out without success, I finally admitted defeat.

Tasha managed to get out of the car once by squeezing herself around the dog guard and getting out of the window that had been left open for her. She has also chewed her way out of one of those soft folding kennels whilst at a dog show. I had her son Jack in the ring and was met by a young girl as we came out who had recognised her running around and had put her on a lead for me. None of the others have really given the bid for freedom so much effort. When put in something, be it pen or a kennel, they have just accepted it and waited for me to let them out. Not my Tasha.

She also escaped out of the garden whilst I was at work and gave all the neighbours the run around trying to catch her before Nell who lived next door realised what they were all doing, and she had my work number. I came home straight away, but she had already been captured and Nell and her sister were looking after her. She and the others were outside because I was working in Boston so I had set them up so that they could get into the rear door of the garage for shelter if it rained, and also have the run of the top yard. She had found a way out, heavens knows where, and I had not got time to look for how just now, that would have to wait until later, so I put them in the house and went back to work. I would have to investigate when I came home at night. As a neighbour pointed out it could take weeks to find her escape route. The best way to do so is sit and watch them without them knowing if possible and wait for them to try it again. But there is no time limit on how long you may be waiting.

She is by no means the only dog to escape. My Granddad's dog Judy had disappeared one morning. I had gone over there as I was going out with him on a bike ride, I used to like going with him round all the local farms, I felt really self important walking in to the big farm yards and talking to the farmers, well my Granddad did all the talking, I just stood there listening. Some of them used to acknowledge me as ask if "was alright" which in Lincolnshire speak meant "Hello". After a short time I just got bored and wanted to get on with the ride, but my Granddad could "chat the hind leg off a donkey" about nothing really interesting, not from my perspective anyway. On my first ever real ride with him as he taught me how to ride a bike in the first place, we went down to this farm just over a mile from home and it took nearly all afternoon because I kept stopping to look at things on the way. Years later when I was into serious cycling, I was a lot older then, I did the same trip in less than three minutes.

He was calling Judy and got no response; and after a while of calling and still no response he went up and down the road on his bike looking for her. They lived down a dead end road and cars never drove very fast down there, and in those days there were very few of them, only half the people who lived down there owned one and most of those that did were out at work all day. While Judy was kept in generally, she would take herself off sometimes given half a chance. After nearly an hour of calling and searching, still no dog, and by this time he was getting pretty annoyed with her because he wanted to go out and time was getting on. I eventually found her, by chance, head first in a very large hole she had dug under the hen house. My Granddad was not best pleased as he had to stay behind and fill it in, and she had been digging for over an hour. The hole was that big she was nearly invisible when she was stood in it, and this was why it had taken us so long to find her. So that was the end of the trip out, because by now dinner time was fast approaching.

Another time my Granddad was out in the yard making an eel trap from a wooden frame to which he was attaching chicken wire. He was using U shaped tacks to do this. He had gone indoors to watch a horse race he wanted to see and while he was gone Judy spied the paper bag these tacks were in and took them into the kennel and into her straw bed before pulling the paper bag to pieces. She did nothing with the tacks she just wanted the bag. Dogs seem to take great delight in pulling paper bags to pieces. When he came out and found the bag was missing it did not take him too long to put two and two together. He then had to go on his hands and knees with a magnet to try and retrieve them all from Judy's straw bedding. I thought it was funny. He was not amused.

These were the "good old days" when things went along in their own time. On those long hot summer days, full with buzzy bees playing in the wide open flowers. Lazy days, when time and tide didn't matter, and one of those large thistle seeds drifted along on the gentlest breath of a breeze.

Chapter Thirteen

Despite his difficult start to life Jack went from strength to strength. He was a bit timid to start with around the others and they used to pinch his food off him given half a chance. To stop this I started to feed him in a cage and used to close the door behind him until he had eaten his food, and to this day he still has his food in there, but now with the door left open because woe betide anyone that goes near him now while he is eating, and he usually finishes first anyway. He keeps all his treasures in their as well, he has that many bits and bobs in there sometimes there is hardly room for him, and he will stand watching anxiously as I take some of the clutter out. (Sorry Jack – I mean treasures).

He particularly enjoys tearing small boxes to pieces and takes them in there so that the others cannot pinch it off him and guards all the pieces jealously. He also likes to play with the cardboard tubes out of the kitchen roll when it has finished, and every time he sees me with the kitchen towel he will stand there hoping that it will be the last sheet. It is a good job his brother is not interested because I don't think he would get a look in. Jack will take a tube upstairs with him if he can find one at bed time, and then station himself under the bed either pulling it to shreds or keeping any potential poachers at bay. Sooty and Sweep used to like playing with these, and what I had to do with them was save a finished one and keep it out of sight until there was another one available. All my work colleagues used to save theirs for me. Despite there always being two they still wanted the same one. They were the same with their food, about half way through they both had the idea to try the one next door, and swapped to each other's bowls simultaneously, and miraculously they somehow never actually clashed with each other. This had to be stopped when they were grown up and fed slightly different amounts, because Sooty as the smaller dog did not need quite as much as Sweep. Maybe she would not agree, but that was just tough.

The larger number of dogs you keep the more difficult keeping the peace between them becomes, it can be worse than trying to run the United Nations sometimes. Who needs to be fussed first on my return, who should be fed first, who should be first through the door when they are all coming in together for breakfast. Ideally the leader should be me, and it is important to maintain that authority or there is always one of them ready to try and take control if the slightest chink in my armour becomes apparent.

Just like two brothers, Jack and Arran argue, they fight and bicker between themselves. But I don't think they would be parted now. Not for long anyway. Jack is the more cautious of the two. Arran has a kamikaze attitude to life. When they first went to the beach, he was straight in to the sea up to his tummy, until the first wave came in and soaked him. On one occasion he was actually swept up the beach because he was engulfed by this extra large wave which I did not see coming until it was too late to do anything about getting him out of the way. It was like his personal little tsunami and luckily for him he was on an extending lead. He spent several days thereafter shaking his head because he must have got water down his ears. It didn't deter him though because two minutes later after giving himself a shake off, he was back in splashing around as if nothing had happened. Jack tends to keep himself out of the water until he has got the measure of the tidal flow, and is quite happy to paddle around in the shallow bits. Niki being even more cautious, walks well up the beach and well away from any possible tidal surge.

The beauty with sand is that unlike mud which sticks like glue forever to the fur, when the dog dries out it just falls off the animal. All into the car boot and the carpets, but the point here is it doesn't stick to the dog! Very handy if the dog has been bathed and groomed ready for a show the next day, and the salt spray can help enhance the coat, it works for them anyway.

A walk on the shore line can also hold other advantages. The sound of the waves is very therapeutic, or I find them to be, I don't know if it has the same effect on the dogs. But even if it doesn't Toby, just like Arran, certainly enjoys splashing in the surf. There is nothing more relaxing on a bright winters morning as the tide is out and the sun reflecting on the wet sand, than an hours walk on a quite beach, because all the holiday makers are at home, probably still in bed. This to me is the best time of the year to be on a quiet beach, with two dogs splashing around and dodging the waves. They always sleep well after a walk up the shore front. It works for me too.

As puppies, Jack and his brother helped themselves to a ten pound note that must have fallen on the floor, and tore it up into tiny little pieces. I picked them all up and after half an hour's work with a roll of sellotape all the pieces were there bar a very tiny piece about two millimetres square. The bank accepted it to swap for a crisp new note. The bank clerk said "Oh dear," when I told her why I was handing her a dilapidated tenner, that was not quite the term I used and is not repeatable here, but roughly translated, meant the same.

Being the least adventurous of the two, the worst Jack has managed so far is to venture down a steep sided dyke after a dog on the other side, and when he got stuck in the water and couldn't climb out decided to then start shouting for help. The lady with the dog on the other side tried to coax him up towards her, but that was just as steep. She didn't want me to go down because she said I would fall in. But what else could I do? I inched my way down using tufts of grass as handholds until I got to the lip above the water and then reached over to hoist him out by his collar. Once back on the bank and terra firma he was able to scrabble up to the top on his own. And no, I didn't fall in!

I have had to rescue Toby on more than one occasion from the water because while he can swim naturally the banks can have overhangs that he is unable to negotiate. As a young puppy he took a dive into the river after a duck before I could stop him. The duck just took off before he got to it, and when he swam back he could not get over the wooden quay that had been put there to stop the bank eroding. He wasn't that old or big either so he had to be lifted out, again by the collar. I don't like them swimming in rivers and discourage them all from doing so because for starters I cannot swim very well. I could scramble out if I fell in but would not volunteer to get in. One night when out walking a dog there was a Labrador caught in reeds in the centre of the river on a very wide sweeping bend. A little lad stood on the nearby bridge bawling his eyes out because his dog was in trouble, whilst his Dad was doing his best to get to his dog. He fortunately made it and saved the animal. But this just goes to show that even the biggest of dogs can get themselves into trouble. The things we do for dogs.

When Toby gets out of the car, it is a bit like launching an unguided missile, definitely unguided. He also has a kamikaze attitude so I can see where Arran gets it from (despite Toby not having any direct influence in the breeding of said dog). He needs to be pointed in the right direction before I open the car boot or else I will not see him for dust, and before I know where I am he can be a quarter of a mile down the road before he notices I am not with him and comes hurtling back to see where I have got to. I would love to put him against a greyhound just to see for how long he could hold his own in a race, because when I open the car boot it is a case of stand clear and that flash of black was Toby. When they all used to go out together, all three boys would try to outdo each other. Jack, being the smallest is always last, but this is not going to deter him from trying his best every time. Tasha and Niki could not be bothered to even try.

On a cold, cloudy and windy but otherwise pleasant morning in March, I had Toby and Tasha out, I had seen sense by now and walked them in two groups, with a smaller number it made controlling them a whole lot easier. Toby had strayed down the bank on several occasions and onto the farmers land, in his usual selective hearing manner he did not respond to being called back and I had had to go and fetch him back. It was when we came to the point behind Surfleet Reservoir where we normally turned round that I first noticed the car keys were missing. And as you do when this happens, I went through all my pockets several times frantically checking for them. All the way back I searched for them. The grass was fairly short, but I didn't find them. They could be anywhere and not necessarily on the path. It's funny how when you drop something it seems to disappear into a black hole.

When I have the dogs with me I never lock the boot down properly, because unless someone comes along carrying a certain sized spanner, they cannot get into the rest of the vehicle because of the dog guard. In the glove box is a spare key to the car. Probably not the best of ideas from a security point of view, but right now it was becoming an ever better idea by the minute. So I looked round for something to break the side window with and found a half brick. I chose a rear window because being non electric it should in theory be cheaper and easier to replace? There are probably a lot of mechanics out there shaking their heads at this point. Anyway, when you see this done on TV it is just a quick smash of the glass and you're in. Not in this case. On the first attempt the brick actually bounced off the glass, I had chosen the spot nearest the window frame as that is supposed to be where the glass is the firmest, a policeman told me that. Thinking I needed to try harder I hit the glass harder several times before the brick broke in two in my hand. The glass - hardly marked.

There was a farm house just down the road, so I put the dogs in the boot and closed it down gently so as not to lock it, and walked towards the farm. I had decided that if I could borrow a spanner I could get the dog guard down and get into the car that way. Fortunately someone was at home and as she answered the door looked young enough to know what a millimetre was. I had visions of some deaf old dear answering the door who would not have any idea what a spanner was let alone the size of one so that was a relief, because sometimes in situations like this you just know you are on a hiding to nothing and may as well give up before you get started.

Anyway she lent me her husband's socket set which she found in the garden shed, because to begin with she was not too certain where they were because he had been using them to do some work recently. When I got back to the car I tied the dogs to the towing hook with their leads while I took the bolts out of the dog guard fixings and climbed in over the back seat for the spare car key. We were in business.

Chapter Fourteen

Sooty was always a healthy little dog and only saw her vet at best once a year, apart from the year grass seeds were in abundance and before I found out about the snood ear covers you can get for them. She kept looking off colour and then as right as rain by the next morning, and what was wrong with her was difficult to put a finger on. Anyway in the end I whisked her to the vet one morning before she had time to look better again, and the upshot was they kept her in to do some tests. She was now nine years of age, the expected life span of a cocker is around twelve, so it came as a shock when the vet told me when I phoned at 3pm to see if she could come home that she had chronic liver failure and she had not got long to live. In a numb state of disbelief at what I had just been told I put the phone down and when the news finally sunk in, which took quite a few minutes to absorb; I burst into tears. She was hardly any age, so why her? I couldn't believe it. Although I love them all she was everyone's favourite, she was always the first to go forward fearlessly to greet people and welcomed everyone after initially barking at them, as soon as visitors sat down, she would climb up on their knee and go to sleep. Sooty liked everyone and everyone liked Sooty. When she wagged her tail at you she did not just move her tail her whole backside got in on the act. She would particularly like to sit on Nell's knee when she came round from next door for a cup of tea and a chat. When Nell found out she was even more upset than I was, and she was my dog. Sooty was the boss and all the other girls respected that, so there were never any real disputes over the top spot it was just accepted as her's.

I went to fetch her home, still numb from the devastating news. As I went to pick her up she was pleased to see me as usual. There was also some special food for her to be started on immediately, and she would have to go back next morning for a further injection.

She rode home in the passenger seat of the car as she liked to do. This is neither recommended nor legal, but I knew she would just sit there and behave, and she did. She lay there beside me as good as gold all the way home. When we arrived home it was tea time. She wolfed down her new food, nothing wrong with her appetite then, and at least she liked it.

Next day I took her to the vet for her injection. The vet we saw stressed to me that we were fighting a losing battle here and that she was not going to get better. I said I was well aware of this, but whilst she was not in any pain and they were happy to allow her to, then I wanted to go on with her as long as possible. I had taken the afternoon off work to take her on one of her favourite walks. I did this for the full fortnight of the rest of her life. She did not want to walk as far or quite as fast as she usually did, but this did not matter, what was important was making each day as happy and enjoyable as possible as it may be her last. This went on until one Monday morning, she had made it to the bottom of the road when she turned and looked at me as if to say "I have had enough now." Right that was it; I always said that the day that dog could not go for a walk would be the time to call it a day, because she would not pass up the chance of a walk for anything. I didn't want to, but phoned the vet and asked if Julia could put her to sleep. I wanted Julia to give her her last injection because she had given her her first. The receptionist told me to bring her at half eleven.

When we arrived the waiting room was deserted, and it was not at all easy sitting there waiting to be called in. Sooty climbed up on my knee and just sat there as good as gold while she waited. All I wanted to do was get out of there and drive away, somewhere, anywhere. But she was not well and could not go on any longer. It was my duty to do my best for her, and at this moment in time this was the only and the best thing to be done. I had pre arranged with Julia that I wanted to have her cremated, and had asked her to make a note of this because when it came to it I might not be able to tell her. Sooty continued to sit calmly on my knee, as she always did when she went to the vets. Not suspecting anything.

Or was she aware of what was going to happen and just accepted the situation, and sat calmly because she knew she was here to be made better? Who knows what they can sense. I say this because when we had Lucky put to sleep, the vet came out to her, and when he arrived she welcomed him, something she would not have done normally, because she knew he was there to help her?

When we were called in, I told the vet that I thought we had reached the end of the road with her, unless she wanted to tell me otherwise. She said that if I had reached that decision on my own then she was happy to go along with it; she added that if she thought Sooty had another fortnight to go she would tell me, but she said it would be only a matter of days at the most. Hardly able to speak I nodded and Julia went to fill a syringe. So with the help of a vets nurse, Julia cut the fur from Sooty's arm; who just sat there, so trusting. I held her and kissed her, trying not to be too upset for her sake. The needle was inserted into her arm and the plunger pressed down. The last voice she heard was mine as I whispered to her as she passed quietly away.

Within seconds Sooty collapsed and that was the end, she had gone. I laid her out straight because she had fallen awkwardly with her legs crumpled underneath her, removed her collar and left.

This is a beautiful, peaceful and painless way to go.

Just like passing away in your sleep.

It was not an easy thing to do and it is no easier now all this time later sitting here writing this, and it doesn't get any easier. But the dog has given you its whole life of unconditional love and devotion, and this is the final act of kindness you can do for your faithfully loyal companion who has always been there for you no matter what.

I had wondered how the others would react, now she had gone, they did not seem too concerned and did not appear to look for her, almost as if they knew. Niki sat in Sooty's usual chair as if to take the top spot that Sooty had held up to now, Sweep had never been interested in the Alpha position. So that was sorted fairly amicably.

This may sound silly and the sceptics will argue that it is my imagination, but it was whilst dozing in bed one morning a few days later that I heard Sooty bark, and I knew it was her and not any other dog without any shadow of a doubt. I can pick her bark or any of my dogs out of a million, it was as if she was letting me know that she was okay now.

Sweep went on for a further two years, to the week to be exact. Read into that as a coincidence what you like. Out of all five of them their birth dates are also within four days of each other, the eighteenth, twentieth and twenty-second. I had vowed I would get Sweep to great grandMother-hood, and succeeded, even if it was only by two months. She developed a large cataract on her right eye and was totally blind on that side in her latter months of life, but sight is not the primary sense for a dog and they will enjoy life quite happily despite any lack of vision. It could have been operated on, but at her age the risks were too great and the stress it would put her through, her vet was happy to leave it. She went out for a walk with her daughter so that she had another confident dog at her side to guide her, and Niki would walk slowly with her at Sweep's pace, looking bored, but happy to assist.

Sweep was put to sleep from failing kidneys after spending a week at the vets on a drip. I went to see her every day, and it was on the Friday that Julia said she was not going to get better. They had tried to get her to eat on her own, and although she had rallied round for a bit, she had relapsed again and it was only the drip that was keeping her alive right now, and Sweep kept pulling that out in the night given half the chance. Julia said I could bring her home if I wanted, but I would be back on Monday morning. I had to make a decision quickly and decided that it would not be fair on Sweep to ask her to go on, or to put her through the journey home only to have to bring her back again. I asked if I could see her and spend some time alone with her. They brought her through having taken the drip tube off her, but had left in the connection into the vein. Julia left us alone.

After spending a few moments on our own I hugged her and kissed her, she responded kissing my face, she still recognised me, so she was not completely out of it. She wagged her tail as she continued to lick my face. Again I did not want to do this next bit, but it has to be done despite how sad it is and regardless of what I wanted to do. I went to the door and opened it and reluctantly went out into the reception area indicating to Julia that I was ready. I was asked if I wanted to stay, I pointed out that if she was going to die, she would do so in my arms not in a stranger's. Julia came and put her to sleep. I stayed with her and lowered her down gently as she collapsed into unconsciousness. She was gone.

She has rejoined her sister in a casket on top of the chest of drawers in the bedroom; both have their individual collars on top, together with some of their best rosettes from shows past.

They are both free and at peace now.

Chapter Fifteen

With a dog time alone is a rarity. One time when I had left Sooty and Sweep with my parents while I went out somewhere, on return I had gone home first to drop off whatever. Just being in the house without another living soul, and no dogs under my feet, it was so quiet; a real novelty and so peaceful, a rare moment that very seldom occurs, and I have to guiltily admit that I stopped and had a cup of tea to saver the peace and quiet before I went to fetch them. Mind you, it was just a little too quiet, that only needed to last briefly, I was already missing the usual hubbub they caused. So when an only pet is no longer there it can be more than some can cope with. And my advice to anyone in this situation would be to find a replacement as soon as possible. Others feel that this is not exactly respectful to the one just departed, and you have to go with what you feel comfortable with, but it helped me get through having the others around. When we lost Lucky we had said no more. Within three months we had Dixie, a Shetland Sheepdog. However when you have several there is very little time to reflect on the loss, although it is still heart breaking and sad, those that remain act as a distraction because they still need to be fed and taken for a walk. They do seem to notice for a day or two that one is missing, but their priority is to preserve the equilibrium of the remaining pack. There may be a reshuffle of the pecking order, especially if it was the alpha dog/bitch that has gone; otherwise it is business as usual.

Dogs will follow you everywhere, (and that does include to the little room) and have a nasty habit of walking right behind you. It is like having a permanent shadow, and subconsciously just by stepping back a yelp will emit as he/she whips his/her paw out from under your foot. It is usually the boys because the girls are not quite so clingy. Jack is my worst and he knows just how he can make me feel really guilty if I stand on him by mistake. He gives me the hardest of stares; and no amount of apologising seems to make a scrap of difference, I still did that on purpose!

Another very annoying habit they have is walking just in front of me, and always slowly, usually when I am in a hurry to get somewhere like fetching in the washing if it starts to rain. They seem particularly proficient at doing it when I am trying to get to the phone before the answer machine kicks in or else whoever is calling gives up. At least when someone knocks on the door, they all race round to the gate, and before coming back enters their heads, gives me time to hot foot it to the front door, closing the door into the hall behind me. And why is it that every time I go to the fridge I can guarantee there will be a dog sat in front of it, never the freezer which is not used as often, is the same colour i.e. white and only situated just next door to each other?

When they have anything wrong that they cannot sort themselves, they will look to me to sort it out for them. A dog's trust is unquestioning, particularly when they are in trouble. Toby had a grass seed in the corner of his eye one time and after a few swipes with his paw to try and remove it himself proved unsuccessful, he came to me and let me lift it out using his eye lids to get it off the eyeball and then wipe it away for him. He has also had something stuck to his paw, a bit like us having a stone in our shoe I expect, and he just stood with his paw in the air until I caught him up to take a look.

You do see life while walking the dog. I won't say there is never a dull moment because there are plenty of those at times. Especially when it is howling a gale in the middle of winter, and I am thinking "Why am I doing this?" and wishing I was anywhere else but battling with this force of nature. Strong cold winds are another story. Sooty and Sweep had gone up to Skegness shortly after I had first acquired four wheels. When we arrived it was blowing a gale. The sand was swirling up all over the beach in force ten winds, and to add insult to injury with the wind that was coming straight off the sea, came intermittent heavy showers of rain. It was so bitterly cold; so cold I could count the number of teeth I had in my head purely by the pain that was throbbing from them with the sub zero wind hitting the exposed skin of my face. The dog's were slowly changing colour, because their coats as they became ever wetter in the squally showers, were collecting more and more of the sand that was blowing relentlessly around and sticking to their soaked fur. Yet another of those occasions when I am sure they were convinced I was completely bonkers. (And I am sure these occasions far outnumber how many toes they have to count them on).

Anyway, I digress, so back to the seeing life aspect; Sooty and Sweep had gone all the way down Roman Bank and as we were getting to the point behind Surfleet Reservoir, we were approaching a car that was parked on the bank top. I had seen it from miles back and assumed it was someone fishing. They should not have taken a car up there because it is illegal to drive a motor propelled vehicle along the sea defences, except at a pull over point for farm vehicles. Anyway, as we got closer I could see that they were not fishing, not in the true sense with a rod and line anyway. Sooty had gone in front and was fast approaching the car with a view to putting her paws on the window sill and looking in. Have you ever tried to shout quietly? If not and you own a dog, I would strongly recommend you try, like right now, you never know when it might come in handy. After three or four softly but hissed commands to try and give them emphasis without making too much noise, she thankfully, finally listened, and came back to me without the two love birds on the back seat being aware we were there.

On another occasion I have drawn up to park alongside a couple of other cars already there, and very shortly afterwards, a sheepish looking couple appeared from the other side of the bank, hastily got into their respective vehicles and shot off at high speed, in opposite directions. So no prizes for guessing what they were plotting if not already up to.

Now to another topic. Walking five dogs together on your own is a bit of a no no, especially five lively, self-willed Cockers. I used to take them to places that other people hardly ever went, but this could involve driving round and round for ages to find somewhere suitable where no one else had already beaten me to it, this planet is far too populated at times, and I could never guarantee someone else would not turn up later. Park somewhere remote, the moon for instance and you can guarantee in five minutes someone will draw up behind you. It takes far longer than you think to put five dogs on a lead and a mammothian effort to hold them all, a struggle if not impossible if they all decided to pull in unison because their combined weight is equal to, if not greater than mine. So I needed a different strategy here, especially as Jack and Arran have got to full size and are now heavier and stronger. Now if we are going down the road on leads I take Tasha with Niki. Toby goes on his own, because he is a really strong dog and handling him with another dog on a lead is impossible. Toby is two stone of solid muscle, and it can look embarrassing when I am fighting with him trying to keep him on track and failing miserably. Then Jack and Arran go together, although they can be more than a handful when they spot another dog, and Arran has got binocular vision and usually spots something to chase well in advance of the others seeing it, including me at times, especially if I am day dreaming, and of course that is never the case!

When we go out in the car, Toby and Tasha make up the first party, and then Jack, Arran and Niki in the second. This works fine until Tash comes into season, and then she has to go with her Mother, and Toby and the other two in the second party. I do not like Arran going out with Toby because Arran will copy everything Toby does, and Toby has every bad habit you can imagine, like running off and not responding to the recall. So it is with some relief that Tash has now been spayed and the walking arrangements can remain consistent. Although as time has gone on Toby has quietened down as he has got older, and maybe now he may actually teach Arran some manners when he is out.

Another difficulty with walking all five together is like the time when Tasha found an adder in a clearing in Thetford forest. It was not very lively because it was not a very warm day, but it was still ready to strike at her if the need arose, and adders are poisonous. The problem was getting her away from it and on the move again before the others who had already passed it by totally oblivious to its existence, came back to see what she was finding so interesting. Moving five dogs simultaneously from something of interest, as the adder would no doubt have been, on my own, nigh impossible. Because get one moved and go back for another the first one will already have nipped round behind me and back again. Fortunately they were not paying too much attention to her and were quite some distance in front of us. Toby walked right by an injured Barn Owl once as I held my breath until he was passed it. He did not see it in the stubble as I had not spotted it either until it was too late to do anything about him. Had I called him or distracted him he may then have spotted it as he turned to see what I wanted.

Feeding time is like running a NAAFI kitchen as they are all fed slightly different amounts and the bowls have to be put down in a certain order and in a certain place, otherwise all hell would break loose. There is a well established pecking order, Jack is given his first and he eats in his cage as he has always done since puppyhood. Next and almost simultaneously, Niki, then Tasha and Toby. Their bowls are in a double frame so Tasha and Toby eat side by side; and finally Arran, who waits quite patiently till last, gets his. He has a tendency to dive in with his muzzle and ends up throwing bits of food all over which he then has to scrabble round the floor and clear them up quickly before his brother comes and starts to help himself, Arran also has to get back to his bowl first, else he would lose that to the competition. As time has gone on he has learnt not to go at his food like a bull at a gate, but he still eats far too fast and spends the next hour or so repeating himself because he has bolted his meal. Nine times out of ten he will also end up with hiccups after eating, again due to him scoffing his food down far too quickly, and while the others get them occasionally, he is by far the champion. He will sit there hiccupping away and will try moving to different locations around the room as if he is trying to get rid of them by moving and leaving them behind.

Toby is my boss dog. Built like a brick out house he only has to murmur a growl and the other two boys bow down to him. The only other dog that will stand up to him is his sister Tasha, his Mother Niki does not bother him, and he doesn't bother her. He is a very complex animal to understand and difficult to interpret at times, and there have certainly been some points of conflict as we have both learnt off each other, but we have come through it. He can also be a very sensitive animal, he really liked his nana Sweep, and when she got older he would sit near her at a respectful distance watching her eating and wait until she had finished and moved away from her dish, before he would go to it and finish off what she had not bothered to clear up. He would make sure none of the others went near her either, although on the surface this looked like an act of kindness, I think his motive was a purely selfish one. But at least he left her alone and would sit there and wait for her to move away. The only dog he has had any trouble with was Blue who must have caught him off balance when they were on a walk together; they were play boxing with each other when Blue accidentally knocked Toby over. Now Toby is more than capable of putting a light Sheltie into the middle of next week, but instead he got to his feet just like we do if we fall over something that isn't there, as quickly as possible before someone saw him, and he looked round to check if anyone had, shook himself and moved off quickly before his embarrassment was noticed. Then for weeks after that he gave Blue a respectable amount of space and left well alone.

Some dogs out on a walk will wait patiently beside their owner if you meet someone and stop for a chat. Some will sit down or even lay down after a while and in extreme cases go to sleep. Not Toby. He has worked out that if he makes a noise by barking all the time whilst I am trying to talk, he will get on the move again a lot quicker than if he just waits quietly, because I cannot hear a word that is being said to me so there is no point in trying to hold a conversation. Result!

In sixteen years Toby has been the only dog to actually catch a game bird. Some of the others have come close. Game birds will sit tight till the last possible moment before they decide to take flight, and this has sometimes nearly cost them their lives. The only thing that stopped us having partridge for tea was that Sooty and Sweep were on extending leads and they ran out of lead before they caught the bird. Had they been free it may well have been another story. Sweep came out of the bushes with a pigeon in her mouth once, demonstrating her gundog skills, she had not bitten it, she was just gently holding it. That is what she should do; she should not mark the game at all, and this is why spaniels need to have soft mouths and a soft bite. So this pigeon she had somehow got hold of was still alive, paralysed with fear no doubt, but still alive. I took it off her and put it back under the bushes. It probably died later of shock, who knows, but the point here is Sweep had not killed it.

Toby was hunting in the long grass on his own when he put up a pheasant that jumped up just in front of him, in typical game bird fashion. Only in non typical game bird fashion it failed to gain height and take flight. By that Toby had caught it and had done it far too much damage for it to survive his attack. One of his faults and would not make him a good gundog is that he has a hard bite. The only thing to do was finish it off. I wrang its neck to put it out of its misery. Thinking waste not want not, I put it in a bag and took it home for the pot. The fact that it was out of season did not matter one jot to Toby. I have told him the in season dates for each bird which I found listed in the cook book I was using to find out how to cook it, which I am sure he has taken on board and will observe them in future – not. It was a cock bird and as my Dad said it had probably been injured fighting over a hen bird at that time of the year, and that is why it did not gain height when it tried to get away from Toby. I got a meal out of it, and being as it was his catch, Toby got the lions share of the left overs, the others just about got a taste because they are not the biggest of birds, and that is why they are usually sold as a brace because there is just not enough meat on one bird to make a substantial meal.

My Grandfather's dog Judy nearly did a similar thing with someone's pet rabbit. To Judy a rabbit was a rabbit and colour did not come into it. Fortunately said white rabbit found sanctuary in one of its burrows just in time or it would have been dog meat, literally. The fact that it is some child's Flopsy and Mopsy or Cottontail had nothing to do with it as far as Judy was concerned, and in typical gundog style, she was not listening to any orders given to her to leave it alone.

Keeping so many and having two that look alike I have not turned up at the vets with the wrong dog yet, but it is no doubt on the cards for some time in the future, in a moment of haste in the mayhem that occurs when trying to separate a specific dog, and there are plenty of those to choose from, I will admit to having to stop down the road and check before now to make sure that the dog in the boot is the one I want with me. I have made the mistake when one of the girls was in season of letting her out with the entire dog and only noticing five minutes later which is quite long enough for things to have happened in the bedroom department, and is not helped if it is dark searching with a torch in a large garden for two specific black dogs.

With four, five even six dogs at any one given time things get worn out or ruined beyond repair four, five even six times as fast compared to someone who only keeps one. (Or to put that another way even faster than someone who has the foresight not to own a dog in the first place!) This is not a go at the Cocker specifically; potentially this goes for any breed. Carpets, beds, furniture, you name it, it is all vulnerable to attack from teeth and claws, especially with young puppies, which leads indirectly to an attack on your finances as the ruined item(s) need to be replaced. The worst Sooty and Sweep did was chew a tiny piece of carpet near the front door. Tasha and Toby decided to pull the zip off one of the bean bags in the night and the bedroom looked like a blizzard had struck as there were those tiny little polystyrene balls all over the place. They won't vacuum up because they become static-ized and they have to be picked up one by one. There must be zillions in one bean bag as I was still finding them months later. And Tasha on her own is a little sod for chewing anything left in her reach. She did stop it though after having her litter of pups. Jack will try to demolish the fitted carpet in the car boot if left on his own for any length of time in there. He has chewed through the rear seat belts twice to date. He will also take the connection for the brake lights out, so there I am going down the road with no rear lights.

Their colour black has been the cause of other problems in various ways, particularly when it is dark. I have fallen over Sweep whilst out on a walk before now as she stopped in front of me up a dark alley, and the next I knew she was there was when she emitted a yelp as I stood on her paw or something, it was dark and I couldn't see her or exactly which part of her I had managed to stand on. The council have since put a street light in there now, but somehow I don't think Sweep's protest had much clout in influencing that decision. When such accidents happen they look at you because you did that on purpose and do not seem to appreciate that they are black and in the dark they become invisible. They can see better in the dark than we can and probably assume that we can see the same as they can, so there may be some logic to their theory. Another time was when there was a power cut one dark morning in winter, and that torch that is always on the bedside table was nowhere to be found, not in the dark. Typical that. So I had to wait for daybreak before I dare get out of bed, because scattered somewhere around the floor were five black and invisible dogs. In defence of blacks though, they don't show the muck so easily and their hairs do not show up round the house like white ones do. Also with blacks if you make a mistake trimming them, their coats are so profuse that any error will have grown out again in a day or two.

When showing you are always asked by the judge how old the dog is and I have had to think before now for a moment "now which one are you?" and then quickly tot up just how old the exhibit is. Their papers, like their vet's vaccination certificate and all their registration documents are kept in individually named folders to make it simpler when they go for their annual inoculations, I just have to grab whoever's folder instead of searching through half a dozen certificates. They all have their vaccinations in groups of two at different times of the year which makes it less of a financial headache at any one given time.

Visits to the vets can be a nightmare with an un-cooperative dog that is likely to snap first and ask questions later. Toby has to be muzzled as a precaution because he will not take any prisoners. Sooty on the other hand would just sit there and let them do anything to her. She had an ulcer on her eye one time and when she went back for a check up to see how it was responding to the application of drops she had been prescribed, the vet wanted to try rubbing it with a cotton bud. She put an anaesthetic in her eye to numb it and when it had been given time to take effect Sooty just sat there as good as gold while the vet rubbed the cotton bud over her eye. So trusting, despite having stayed with the vet for previous operations, which usually puts them off even going near the place ever again. If she was going to stay for the day she would just walk off with the vets nurse, not even looking back, she would even turn in the right direction from the door; she knew where the cages were. That is one thing that makes this breed so easy to steal; they will just go off with anyone. It would not be the first time when passing someone going the opposite way, to turn round and find that one or other of them was walking off in the opposite direction with whomever, despite not knowing them. Tasha had gone down the side of a bank once, and when she finally came back up she went galloping off after the first person she saw who happened to be walking in the distance, and it was not until she nearly got to him that she realised her mistake and came galloping back again.

Chapter Sixteen

Niki was not looking herself on the Monday morning, so I took her to the vets just to confirm it was nothing. She had been two months earlier for a check up; they had taken a sample of blood and found nothing wrong then, so I was expecting the result of this visit to be the same.

How wrong could I be? The vet who saw her found a heart murmur which she said it was quite loud, so that had come on in the last two months. She was also stiff in her back legs so she gave her a course of pills to help her joints and also some to try and rectify the heart murmur. She wanted to see her back again in a weeks time to see how the tablets were working.

We didn't get to the week. Come the Wednesday she was back again. Her stomach had now swollen up into the bargain. Her vet did not like this and said it did not look good. The heart murmur was now worse, so she gave her a full course of heart tablets, and wanted to see her again the next day.

When she went again the next day she was no better, if anything her swollen stomach was worse. Her vet gave her an injection to try and get the fluid causing the swelling to disperse. She was back again next day, still no better and not eating properly. The first question they ask when you take an animal to the vet is "are they eating?" If the answer is no, something is definitely amiss. The vet intimated that we had probably lost the war here and could only suggest another injection to try once again to disperse the fluid that was causing her stomach to swell.

By Saturday she was no better and would not look at her food. I did not even bother to try and give her her pills because I would have had to force her to take them, and looking at her I began to wonder if I should not just let the vet call it a day. When I phoned the vet the earliest they could see her was not until eleven, and by then she had started to perk up a bit and show an interest in her surroundings and what was going on. The vet gave her another injection and said they would see her Monday.

She came home and was still not interested in food, and it was not until tea time that I managed to tempt her with a bit of chicken, she did not eat a great deal but it was a step in the right direction, she had eaten something. Secretly my hopes began to rise that things might be improving.

Only to be dashed an hour or so later when she went outside and promptly brought the chicken back, hardly digested. I was going to have to face up to the fact that it was not worth going on with this for her sake, and come Monday morning I was going to have to let the vet put her to sleep.

Later in the evening Niki trundled her way outside and went to sleep underneath the garden bench, so I left her there; it was a warm night so she would be okay. I kept looking at her and she was just sleeping, peacefully.

When I next went to look at her and to fetch her in as it was her bed time, she didn't move as I approached her. As I got closer and touched her, she had already passed away.

I don't know which is worse, having to take them to the vet to be put to sleep, or where they die peacefully in their own home. To begin with I am no expert on dead bodies and you hear such horror stories, recent ones at that, about people who appear dead but are not, and are unable to communicate the fact that they are still alive. I could not hear her breathing, nor find either a heartbeat or a pulse. I brought her inside and found a mirror to check her breathing. That did not mist up and I still could not find her heart beat or pulse, and went to one of the others to check where the pulse was. I did not want to put her outside just in case she was still alive, although I was as certain as I could be she was dead, so I put her in a dog basket and left her downstairs in peace till the morning. Rigor mortis would confirm she was dead by then.

It brought me to thinking about the time when my Grandfather had to take a shot gun to one of his dogs because she had been hit by a train. I was not even thought of, but my Nan had told me about it one time. They lived close to a railway line and the dog, a Cocker called Dandelion or Dandy for short, had got out and gone up onto the track. My Dad still questions to this day what possessed her to go up there. It was suspected she was pregnant and could have explained the unusual behaviour. There is always a special dog in your life and this was my Dad's. She was laid unconscious; she had been hit in the head by the train, but miraculously was still breathing. Someone came and told my Granddad, who reluctantly took his gun and a cartridge with him and with tears in his eyes had no option but to finish her off. Vet care was not what it is today, you sorted your own problems with animals in those days, and in such a situation the result would have ended the same anyway. I don't know if I could have done what he had to do that day, and will forever envy him of his courage, and hope I am never put in such a situation. My Dad vowed to never let himself get as close to another dog again, but that can be easier said than done.

I did manage to get some sleep; because in a way, it was a release for both her and for me; obviously more so for her. The others were not too bothered at that point and came upstairs with me to bed, and did not seem to make anything of what had just happened, or the fact that Niki did not follow them upstairs as she usually did, they were probably unaware at this point that anything was amiss.

The next morning, she was as I had left her, only now cold and stiff. I removed her collar and nearly jumped a mile as she groaned; apparently this is normal because of gases escaping if you move a dead body. But for a few moments it was unnerving. The others sniffed at her and were bemused about what they were presented with. Toby in particular came to me and buried his head in my chest and whimpered. I tried to reassure him and covered the body with a towel to try and hide her from him. No one can tell me he was not aware that something was amiss or do not have any feelings because he was definitely upset by what had happened. I tried to reassure him as best I could. They say animals are not aware of death and live for the moment, but I am not so sure.

While they were eating their breakfast and were otherwise occupied I moved the body outside and put her on the picnic table out of their way. With it being a Sunday I would have to wait for a decent hour before I phoned the vet, because I wanted her to be individually cremated like I had done with Sooty and Sweep, and they had handled all the arrangements then so I had no reason to want to try elsewhere.

I waited until nine o'clock before phoning to see if someone was going to be in and if I could take the body round, as the weather had predicted it was going to be the hottest day of the year so far. The vet on duty was the same vet that had been dealing with her anyway, so I didn't have to go into details to explain the situation which made things easier. She would be in later that morning, so would take the body in and make all the necessary arrangements. These things never happen conveniently during opening times, not with animals involved they don't. She had dragged the vet out on a Sunday when she was born, so true to form she was going to do the same on her departure.

The period where the body is away and the return of the ashes can be at least a week as the corpses are collected every Monday, so she would have gone more or less straight away. It is a weird interval because you feel that you cannot settle back into normal life until you have done with them what you intend. In my case that will be to put her on top of the chest of drawers in the bedroom alongside where Sooty and Sweep reside. I feel that with cremation you have a choice of what you can do with the ashes. You can bury them, scatter them or keep them. You also have the option of being able to take them with you if you move house, where as if the body is buried in the garden it usually has to stay there, and the new owners may not respect the grave as you have done. I found a cross at the back of the large conifer tree when we moved here. I have left it alone. It is obviously the grave of someone's beloved pet.

It was also with her departure that it put the affinity I still felt I have to Sweep, through her, a generation further back. Towards the end she looked so like her Mother that I subconsciously kept calling her "Sweep". As she got older she also began to adopt so many of her Mother's mannerisms. Certainly while out on a walk she had for a few years now always walked behind, taking her time, going at her pace, I was always having to keep calling her on because she was taking so long over a scent she had found, and then she would suddenly come galloping on to catch up with us because she had became oblivious to just how far behind she had got whilst she was investigating that interesting smell. And it would also take her an age to mark a scent before moving on like it was so important not to waste her time just marking anything and everything, it had to be right. Sweep to a T.

I was going to have to be careful with the others for the next few days, especially Toby whom this seemed to have affected the most. He was the same when Sweep went. It affected him more than any of the others and he really missed her. He was not as close to Niki but seeing the body seemed to have upset him emotionally. I was going to have to avoid shouting at him for any misdemeanours and just be more tolerant towards him for at least the next few days. Despite his tough exterior and the fact that he is the alpha male, he is a very sensitive animal at heart.

I think Tasha also found it strange, she was now the only bitch in the house, and she had always cuddled with her Mother to sleep and they could always be found together wandering around the garden. For a few days she seemed at a loss. You hear these stories of a remaining pet pining so badly after the one that has gone, that in some cases it results in the second one following on very shortly. Tasha did not seem quite that upset, but she definitely missed her Mother and it took her several days to get over it.

And not only had we lost my first born, Mother and grandMother to the remainder, but also their time keeper. Whereas I thought that they could all tell what time it was from the striking of the cuckoo clock, it would seem that they were not all looking at each other for guidance on whether it was feeding time or not when it went off, but they were all looking at Niki who seemed to know instinctively when it was time and was guiding the others, because now she had gone, they just do not have a clue.

Another weird thing is that I have not heard from her after her departure, like I had by this time from Sooty and Sweep. Whether this has anything to do with her passing away naturally whilst the other two had been put to sleep is anyone's guess. Dogs and their actions are sometimes a complete mystery, who knows what goes on in their heads, what they are capable of sensing that we can't. At the end she could be found laid in all manner of strange places that she normally just did not bother with, as if she was looking for somewhere to die in peace. I found her several times in the most unusual of places, laid with her head tucked away from the outside world.

Several weeks after her departure, I think it was more peaceful for her to die at home. At least she went when she was ready and in a place that she was familiar with. Unlike Sweep who spent her last few days at the vets in a strange kennel and unfamiliar surroundings, which may have stressed her with all the other strange animals around her, and all the other comings and goings throughout the day. I hope she was not too upset because it was the best place for her. Niki looked so peaceful as she lay there under the bench. Death is a strange state, so peaceful in some ways and yet violent in others. This as the former, whilst tragic, was a serene passing.

It has been an honour and a privilege to have brought her into this world and to have cared for her, until her choosing of her time for her departure. The bond between a man and his dog is something exceptionally special. A bond that has robustly withstood the test of time and all its changes.

Postscript

And so to the future. Whatever that may be, the plan now is to get another bitch in to put her to Jack when she is ready to be mated, and continue to the next generation. Jack is a super little dog and I would love to have a pup sired by him. He has a great little character which brings together so much of his ancestry. He is a determined little dog who will not stand for any nonsense from no one. Over-willing to please but stubborn in his quest to have his own way over and above all else. Every breeder and show enthusiast have one favourite dog in their lifetime, and because of his difficult start to life, and what it took to get him into gear as it were, he will always be exceptionally my very special little boy.